blue
rider
press

POUR ME A LIFE

ALSO BY A. A. GILL

A.A. Gill Is Away
The Angry Island: Hunting the English
Previous Convictions: Assignments from Here and There
Table Talk: Sweet and Sour, Salt and Bitter
Paper View: The Best of the Sunday Times *Television Columns*
A.A. Gill Is Further Away
Here & There: Collected Travel Writing
To America with Love

POUR ME A LIFE

A.A. GILL

BLUE RIDER PRESS
New York

blue
rider
press

An imprint of Penguin Random House LLC
375 Hudson Street
New York, New York 10014

Copyright © 2015, 2016 by A.A. Gill
Originally published by Weidenfeld & Nicolson

The mission statement of *Parade* magazine is reprinted by permission
of *Parade*, part of the Athlon Media Group.

ISBN 9780399574917

Printed in the United States of America
1   3   5   7   9   10   8   6   4   2

Book design by Lauren Kolm

*Penguin is committed to publishing works of quality and integrity.
In that spirit, we are proud to offer this book to our readers;
however, the story, the experiences, and the words
are the author's alone.*

For the friends of Bill

POUR ME A LIFE

Wake up! You're at sea, it doesn't matter which sea, it's just the sea rising and falling. Sea-flavored, sea-shaped, wet sea. You're in a boat, a little boat—you're alone in a little boat. There is nothing else in the boat but you. The boat bobs. You bob. You have no idea how you got here. This, at least, is not unusual. You woke up in a boat on a sea alone. You look along the horizon, it's as sharp as a razor cut. There's nothing but sea and the cloche of the sky, the salty bobbing earth curving away . . . and then there is something just there, there where the sun makes the water flare and shimmy. There are two dots. Two things that aren't sea, they're boats. Now there are three boats in the sea. These other boats have a purpose, they have come for you and that is the nature of these things, these instructive fables. The inner narrator tells you that though they are coming solely for you, you can stop only one. And to help you choose which, the chorus adds that on the one boat there is a man who will give you food, fresh water, some oars and directions to get to land, and he'll even come with you if you like, but in the other boat there is only a bloke who if you ask him will tell you how you got here. So that's the dilemma—which boat do you stop?

We're back in a room in a private mental hospital in the west of England. They call it a treatment center. This is where you can get treatment. Really, it's a mental hospital—we're mental. That's why we need treating, we're dying. Everyone's dying, of course, but we know it, we can taste it, metallic in our sticky condemned stumpy mouths. We know we're close to the shuffling end of the coil and it's our fault, we caused it, we caused it on purpose, we chose the way of our deaths, we can smell it in the damp corruption, our breathless musty mortality. It lingers in our jackets, on the blankets, in our sad evacuee suitcases. This morning, the doctor holding a file said, "Have you stopped drinking?" Yes, I said. "Are you sure?" he said, giving me the look, the look of nonjudgmental disbelief that is the facial uniform of mental treatment. Yes, I said, yes. We say yes a lot—it doesn't mean yes, it means stop asking me questions. "Yes? Good. Because I've got your tests back . . . and if you go on, you probably won't see Christmas."

I'm thirty. Outside the window there is the sea of green lawn, with croquet hoops, rolling down past trees. I remember them as cedars, huge and lost, standing outside this white classically country house. How easily the architecture of the aristocracy lends its aspirations to the infirm and the insane. Perhaps I've imported cedars—maybe they're from some other rolling lawn. I get lawns confused. Lawns just lie there with a permanent ennui, a sickly languor. I wonder what the rest of nature makes of a lawn. Arrogant, snobbish, entitled, needy, effortfully polite, sober. Rebuke of the wild.

We're here because we're dying. Death presses up against the broken mirror, death stands in the corner of the bedroom, signals from the blood in the bog, the pus in the sock, the tingling in the fingers. It wasn't death that terrified us into this preposterously genteel bedlam with its contrite normal lawn. It isn't the winnowing flail of mortality that grabbed us by the scruff and dragged us all here. Understand this, it's not death that terrifies—it's life. Life is the horror, the unbearable living. We are suffering from life trauma . . . the miserable, shambling, boring, self-pitying lives we have fashioned for ourselves, alone, with shaking hands and a tearful despair.

"So which boat would you stop?" The counselor is a young man, a knowing public school compassionate man. I try to imagine his life but can't. Why would you be here if you weren't mad or carrying the dead weight of a chronic life? Why frolic in the bleak mere of others' troubles posing as a new-life salesman? We listen to him not because he talks compassion or sense but because he's plainly the captain of the boat with the stuff, the gear. We are the people who have run out of choices, run through choices and chances: second chances, last chances, simple choices, choices that were no choice at all. Always wrong, all desperate, always hopeful. Every cast of the bones was a loser. So here's the choice to finally give up on choice; the chance at the far end of choices. There is an infinitesimal lightening in the room like the blowing away of a paper hat, and we choose all together, unanimously. We look at the man with his life so sorted he can spare the time to sell us a new one and we feel ourselves bobbing at sea on a lawn and we shout in our sour-salt tight mouths, "Throw us a line. Give us an oar. Tow us to the further shore, to the new land where we can be whole. Take us where we can wash away this life that we made with the sweat of our face. Relieve us of the dead burden."

This is "Choice Theory." It's a real thing. It was thought up by an American, a psychiatrist called William Glasser who worked in a veterans' hospital in Los Angeles in the '60s. He got fed up with listening to people whine about their lives and regress through their sadness to find the germ of misery in some childish darkness. He decided that what you do is more important than what you did . . . you don't have to scrabble about in a cellar of nostalgia to discover the seed of your madness, just get on with now, do the practical stuff: make your bed, make a list, brush your teeth, brush your shoes, mind your manners, tell a truth, get up, sit up, stand up, own up, call your mother. If your feet point one way, your head can't face the other. They tell us that a lot. This thing is also called "Control Theory" and "Reality Therapy" and "Cognitive Behavioral Therapy." It's a fireman's therapy—a 911 therapy. It's an ax and a ladder, a chance for people who are dying faster than they can talk, who don't have the time or the honesty or the inclination or the words, who don't need any more drugs. It's a cut-to-the-cure therapy. If you behave like a normal nine-to-five guy, then sooner or later you turn into one. Fake it to make it, they say . . . fake it to make it. You don't even have to believe. "Fake it to make it" is a particularly adroit one-size therapy for drunks and junkies because we're already good at faking stuff and we need things to happen pretty pronto. We need a hit. We're not feeling great at the moment. Bill Glasser also believed that there were five things that people needed in order to function properly, and the first and the greatest of these was love. It wasn't an original thought. But they don't tell us this, because frankly no one wants to be told that the answer to everything is love. No one wants the payoff of his tragedy to be the chorus of a pop song.

The night after the last-chance choice, I lie in the dark of a dormitory; there are six or seven of us, no one can sleep. I don't mind sharing a room, I'd been to a boarding school, but the others, the hard boys with scars, they hate it and rant at the propinquity, rage against intimacy. We can't sleep because we're frightened of the dark; of sleeping; of crying out; of blurting; of wetting ourselves; of dreaming. We lie in the cold sweat with the stinking shroud blankets pulled over our faces and feel the self-pity pour into our mouths until we're drowning in regret, and we gasp in panic and in turn tell one another war stories, our voices like distant radios. There's this boy in his early twenties, he's tall but he moves like an old, old man, painfully mistrusting gravity. He's covered in psoriasis and bubbling sores, his nose is bust and his teeth are gone. His body is very close to worn dead. I watched him pack himself into the bed with the slow gentleness of a curator storing ancient porcelain. He has a thick Midlands accent: "I live rough. I've lived rough since I was sixteen. My dad was drunk, my mum didn't like me. I beg and steal for gear. I live in a multistory car park in Birmingham." "Why?" a voice asks from the dark. "Why do you live in a pissy car park? You're a fucking tramp. You can go anywhere, that's the only thing to be said for being a tramp." "Oh yes," the flat vowels answer, "I've got a place in the country as well, a telephone box outside Sutton Coldfield for the weekends." And we start laughing, laughing and laughing and laughing with great wheezing guffaws; laughter that bounces and tumbles off the ceiling and jumps on the beds, billowing the blankets. The noisy, lumpy, hilarious breath runs through me like a great brightness. Magical, free laughter that spins me back to being a child; a hiccuping, chorus-rolling, crashing, howling, sobbing laughter, so unexpected, so strange, like finding that all together we can sing. The tears swim down my cheeks and soak the pillow. Every time the wave recedes someone catches it, pulling us back, sighing, "Outside Sutton Coldfield," not wanting to lose this moment, this marvelous noise. The black dormitory is raucous with small boys who had all their choices ahead of them. That was the moment I knew I had a chance.

Twenty-seven years later I realize that I stopped the wrong boat.

MY FIRST WIFE LEFT ME in the middle of a dinner party. I can't remember what I said or what she said. I don't remember a row or a diagnosis of inoperable discontent. I don't think anything was thrown and I don't know who else was there. Not a single face or name comes back to me, though I remember the detritus, the stained glasses, collapsed napkins, the stricken Stilton; the evidence of a room full of people that remained for weeks like a crime scene or a Spanish still life, a memento mori, the corruption of earthly vanity and fleshly lust. I do remember that we served three sorts of eggs—goose, duck and quail. Why would we offer three eggs? Four if you count a hen's egg in the mayonnaise. Who did we think we were becoming? Offering up dinner parties with napery and Stiltons—it was like charades in the bunker. I suppose, along with goose eggs, it was a sort of married life manqué we hoped we might cobble together out of stuff and things and expectations; out of orphaned china cups and potpourri and Gollancz hardbacks with bacon bookmarks, old, bald velvet and sepia erotica, Charles Trenet and Wallace Stevens and cut flowers out of season in Arts and Crafts vases with broken handles and portrait gallery postcards on a Welsh dresser—did we actually own a Welsh dresser?—and the willful extravagance of a tissue-paper basement bohemianism.

It was never really us. We were us, once. We had been very us, but the life we made out of each other wasn't. So she left because there wasn't anything worth staying for and no prospect of anything worth having or becoming. I knew what she meant. I had every sympathy. If I could have gone with her, I would have—left the marriage behind with the washing up, left it to wilt in the vase, fester with the cheese, watched over by the judgmental curling faces of Christopher Isherwood and Lady Ottoline Morrell.

This story, this memoir, falls between these two events. The three eggs and the phone box outside Sutton Coldfield. It is the year between the end of the marriage and the end of drinking. I say it's a year, but I have no reliable chronology. It might be only six months, or eighteen; it is the space between two ends each looking the other way. To call it a memoir is to imply memory, a veracity, a recall, that I couldn't . . . can't put my hands on. None of this is hand-on-the-Bible fact. The one miserly charity of drink is that it strips away memory. You start by forgetting the last hour of Saturday night, a name, a conversation, how you lost your shoes, and then, as the life begins to tumble like an upended skier, so the avalanche of forgetting comes and sweeps up the evidence, burying the remembrance in a soft white darkness, a roaring silence. After time, you've forgotten more than you can remember. For me, out of a decade I have perhaps two years, perhaps three, of remembrances. Not consecutive, not related or correlated, just images . . . like fragments from sagas found stuffed in a mattress, torn photographs on rubbish heaps, strips of wallpaper painted over that make you wonder at the life that once flourished in your bedroom.

There is a hope, if not a reliable fact, that this is the best I can muster, this is a retrospective truth gleaned from the shards and tesserae. An attempt to reimagine something lost, an emotional archaeology sifting through the midden for a bone, a coin, a few words scrawled on a flyleaf. "My darling, will you . . . ," an earring in a dinner jacket pocket. Without tools or skill, scheme or expectation, this is an attempt to reconstruct, resurrect the boat that was going the other way and its cargo, its log of how I got here. Because frankly the

Choices thing doesn't work the way it used to. Choices beget choices like an infection. I have been sober longer than I was drunk, every day I choose not to drink is now no harder than choosing to wear my shoes on the prescribed feet and having my face point over my toes. It's not the all or the enough, it's not the answer. I am now closer to my last breath than I am to my last drink and I need to know.

But let's get one thing straight, this is no faith-infused pulpit tale of redemption. This isn't going to be my debauched drink-and-drug hell, there will be no lessons to learn, no experience to share, there won't be handy hints, lists, golden rules, you will find no encouragement for those who still stagger. I'm not shifting through this soggy tangle of a shredded life for your benefit, I have no message, no help. This isn't a book to give to your sister whose son is having too good a time, or the friend who struggles with his cravings like a randy fat girl squealing "No, no, no" as her hand shimmies up your shirt.

I MET MY WIFE in The Lindsey Club. A busted sign above a door that opened onto a thin, peely corridor. Under a pale bulb sat Renee. Old. Apparently made by workhouse orphans out of parchment, tannin-stained calico and chicken bones. She was a wisp of a woman who was sustained by cold tea and custard creams. She spoke in a genteel voice that sounded like the responses at Evensong. If she recognized you, she would give you a cloakroom ticket for 50p and you could go on down the stairs. Renee would spend her day comforting and confronting the drunk, the deranged and the damned. She was the most effective bouncer I've ever seen. So delicate and antique, so plainly breakable, that not even the most pugnaciously hammered thug would consider taking it to the mat. I've watched men grab their own collars and eject themselves, screaming that they would go quietly, rather than risk chipping Renee. Murderers would come back the morning after some psychotic outburst, blinking back tears, begging forgiveness, and she would be as stern as a remembrance wreath. Downstairs there was a bald half-size pool table on a tilt, an ancient jukebox that I only remember playing Sinatra crooning "My Kind of Town," a short bar and a mismatched collection of tables and chairs. There were yellow lights with red shades like flung knickers, and a carpet that had the texture of warm tar.

The place was coated with nicotine and despair. It was the most hopelessly sad and lonely room I've ever known. There were glazed windows with curtains, behind which was painted a Home Counties landscape, a wry trompe l'oeil that twisted the truth—we were in a cellar, a burrow, a tomb where the wounded, sodden, failed and frightened came to hide. On the wall there was a reproduction of a painting of eighteenth-century huntsmen enjoying a tale and a tincture in some amiable country hostelry. They were the bucolic English yeomen of yore, ruddy and true, loyal, jolly, prosperous and sturdy. The picture was a slap, a caution, a reminder of how far from the ideal of manhood and society I had fallen. All the coy sentimental attempts to cheer up the bar, tranquilize it with kitsch, the plastic flamenco dancers and china poodles, became the malevolent props of a horror movie.

You handed your ticket to Peggy behind the bar. Peggy was the opposite of Renee. Whatever it was that Renee hadn't eaten for the past fifty years, Peggy had. She was a gargantuan woman, comically, cartoonishly fat, her body apparently made from a series of boiled puddings piled precariously, sagging and falling over one another. She was always reluctant to disturb the distribution of her bulk once it had settled. She would arrange herself over a stool behind the bar and dispense the drinks she could reach—slowly, inexpertly and with prejudice. If forced to maneuver for a particularly unlikely order—a sweet sherry perhaps, or something nonalcoholic—she would breathe deeply through her nose, purse her carmine bow-shaped lips, fix her eye on the object to be retrieved and tense with the effort of propulsion. For a long moment nothing would happen, and then—like a landslide, a bit here and a bit there—she would begin to topple in different directions. Her head would settle like a gyroscope, an arm would wave for balance, and like an elephant crossing Niagara Falls on a unicycle, she would oscillate back and forth, making surprisingly elegant progress until the bottle was reached and she could retrace her trip backward until the safety of the stool would nestle, then gently disappear up her arse.

In the center of Peggy's pale, fleshy, suet-pudding head was a face of great sweetness and jollity. She had an infectious rollicking laugh and a sense of humor whose coarseness transcended its packaging. Aboveground in the daylight, Peggy had been an actress and most memorably the voice of "Weed" in *Flower Pot Men*, a children's TV puppet show that began in the '50s. Weed's role consisted of saying "Weeeeed" with a high-pitched voice in the manner of a daisy.

The third member of the Lindsey staff was Rita, who owned the club. She was also ancient, with a bony, sallow, disapproving face and severely neat hair. Rita was permanently disapproving; she despised her customers as failed, pathetic specimens. She didn't have much time for men if they didn't come with titles or horsewhips. Rita told me I should do better for myself than sit and drink in the Lindsey. She was really the least likely person to run a shabby, subterranean drinking club, but then the Lindsey hadn't always been like this, it too had a past, had aspirations. Once it was a theater club, a soigné stage for amateur and professional rising talent. The young Dirk Bogarde had played the Lindsey, the yellowing poster was here to prove it. But as angry young men and a new realism and swearing claimed the stage, so the Lindsey withered, its bright jollity declining until only the bar remained solvent. And Rita and Renee and Peggy were set adrift in it like a lifeboat come to rest here, beached and broken on this reef of disappointing men.

I loved it. I loved it because it was so perfectly tailored to me—a room I could look in the eye and know that it loved me right back. In exchange for the cloakroom ticket, Peggy would give you a sausage. The Lindsey existed in the crevices of the licensing laws—to drink, you had to eat, and because it was notionally a club, it could serve drink outside opening hours. The Lindsey only really existed between three in the afternoon and five-thirty, and then from eleven p.m. till midnight, which would stretch to one a.m. It was for those for whom the licensed day was not long enough to fit in the required pintage, for those of us who did alcohol overtime. The drink might kill you, but nobody risked eating the sausage: it went to my dog, Lily, a lurcherly mongrel who lived under benches and on sausages. Always ahead of me after closing time at the Elephant & Castle up the road was Alex Trocchi, the Scottish novelist and lifelong junkie. Alex, granite-faced, angry iconoclast, fearless nihilist, rager against the night, had managed to make heroin seem parochial, rather bourgeois. He'd done it for so long that it had become a pomade, a tonic, it never seemed to make any difference to his demeanor. I never saw him gouch or get scratchy. He had a small antiquarian book business and a massive immovable writer's block. Sometimes he'd buy my paintings. We'd sit in corners, him reading fast—a solace and a distraction and I imagine a torture—often with Kit Lambert, son of the composer Constant Lambert and manager of The Who. Kit had had a palazzo in Venice, which he lost or set fire to. He lost everything, including most of the things he tried to put in his mouth. The front of him looked like an abandoned gannet colony. Kit had been arrested for drugs and was convinced that his best defense was to make himself a ward of the court so that the official solicitor gave him pocket money out of his own considerable royalties. Kit looked like a furious French bulldog. He had a voice that sounded like someone continuously trying to start a lawn mower, and he was clownishly clumsy. He could clear a table simply by looking at his watch;

it was all so immensely funny and clever and cultured when he wasn't incoherently drunk. He had an incandescent temper, and if I ever told him to stop setting fire to my clothes or tipping beer into my lap, he'd shout at the top of his mechanical voice, "Oh nanny, nanny, nanny, Gill . . . fuck off." His life had shrunk to a single Herculean tantrum at the parsimony of his executors. The madder he got, the more parsimonious they became. He would conceive ever more absurd ruses to get his money back. He died after being in a fight in a gay club and then falling down his mother's stairs. Alex died of pneumonia three years later. I still have a copy of his *Cain's Book*, inscribed "To Lily, instead of a sausage."

The rest of the Lindsey's customers were art students, diplomatic protection officers—one of whom once pulled his gun on me—mean little criminals, actors, Montenegrin jeans salesmen and Kensington's decrepit and fallen gentry. Men with stinking blazers and burst veins, women who had compacts and cigarette holders and who wet themselves on bar stools. And I seem to remember a statistically significant number of men with nonspecific wounds.

I was sitting under the window, looking out over the Home Counties reading *The Standard*, and a girl standing at the bar slid in opposite me. I'd noticed her because the room was small and there were so few strangers. She was gamine and preternaturally vivacious for the Lindsey. She wore corduroy shorts, lisle tights and a hand-me-down Fair Isle cardigan. She had clever eyes that dodged behind a faded fringe. She said I looked sad. I told her that the girl I was in love with was in New York and I couldn't afford to go to New York, and she couldn't be here, so I was sad. She agreed that that was sad, pulled a large glittering ring off her finger and pushed it across the table. "Take this, I'm sure it's worth a ticket to New York . . . No, really . . . you must take it, go now, go today. It was my great-aunt's engagement ring . . . she was marvelous, had masses of lovers and would simply insist you take it. What on earth are engagement rings for, if not to bring lovers together?" I said I couldn't possibly, but it was incredibly, brilliantly kind of her and it had stopped me from feeling sad and at least I could buy her a drink. I don't even know your name, I said. "I'm Cressida Connolly," she said, sticking out her hand and cocking her head to one side with a grin that was half warm, half defensive, and that I would come to know well. Well, I'm . . . "Oh, I know who you are," she said. Six months later—maybe twelve—she tapped the shoulder of a man in a queue at a baker's and said, "I'm going to marry your son." The man looked askance and replied, "We've never met. How do you know who I am or that I even have a son?" And Cressida cocked her head and grinned: "You could only be Adrian's father."

A few months after that—or maybe weeks—I was lying in a morning bath and she brought me an orphan cup of warm milk and brandy and said, "You know, if we get married, I'll always make sure there's beer in the fridge."

Romantically we peaked too soon.

The DTs—delirium tremens—medical Latin for shaking frenzy. They seem to have gone the way of Gothic fainting, female genital hysteria and poor nerves. They are pre–National Health, a quaint black-and-white starched-wimple rectal-thermometer condition. DTs belong to a nostalgic type of inebriation, along with whiskey bottles with corks, horse-drawn drays and pink gin. I had a summer of pink gins. Drunk as personal self-flagellatory punishment because I was drinking too much; I imagined I'd drink less if the drink was vile. Indeed, they were so gratuitously foul I had to neck the first two at a dead sprint, after which I'd pass caring what they tasted like. The barman always asked, "In or out, do you want the bitters left or flicked?" leaving the gin pale pink–tinctured.

DTs went the way of drunk tanks, straitjackets, padded rooms and music hall drinks. There aren't comedy drunks anymore. There used to be clowns whose acts were slapstick tipsy—stand-up-and-fall-down comedians with semidetached collars, squiffy ties and a broken fag. It was funnier if it was a toff, the descent more precipitous and humiliating, unrestrained by a safety net of sympathy. A flat-cap drunk was a Methodist sermon and a crusade, not a thing of humor; but the posh-pissed are ripe for mockery—the slow mime of misjudgment, the lost keys, the wife in bed with the gamekeeper, top-hatted Johnnies throwing pebbles at lampposts because there's a light on upstairs. When did we stop thinking all that was amusing, why did we stop laughing at drunks? They were such a staple character of John Bullying British humor.

> Before the Roman came to Rye or out to Severn strode,
> The rolling English drunkard made the rolling English road.

The nations of Britain were collated by drink long before they were collected under one crown or church. The brown baritone Welsh drunks, the lyrical Irish drunks, the morose Scots and the tedious English. Boorish, finger-jabby, jut-chinned drunks all of them, nations that are heavy and mild, light and bitter, gin-soaked, whiskey-steeped, cider-soused. Every so often some why-oh-why politician will ask, "Why oh why can't the British drink like the continentals . . . like the southern Europeans?" The question is rhetorical, inspired by the memory of agreeable afternoons spent in the staccatoed buzz of Tuscan villas or provincial village squares listening to the plink-plink of *pétanque* and the drone of fat Englishmen in straw hats. No one ever asks drunks in the dank corners of urban pubs why they drink like dank drunks in dark corners instead of like happy dagos in the sunshine. So we never hear the rhetorical answer, fruity with phlegm and sprayed crisp crumbs—"We drink like this because we can, because it's our birthright, it's our heritage, our history, our myth and legend. Why would you drink like a prissy prancing mellifluous child of Dionysus in the vineyards of antiquity when you could bellow obscene songs in the mead halls of Asgard? We are the chilly, sweaty drunks of the north, of the long nights. We drink in the dark in the flickering shadows, not in the sunny blue-hued shade of the south. We drink like this because we fucking can."

It was the medical Latin that killed the humor of drunks, when they designated alcoholism an illness rather than a weakness or a choice or a culture—that's when it became mocking the disabled. You can't laugh at an illness, an ism, unless you're pissed. But then I never had much time for theatrical lushes; drink was my craft, I took a professional pride, and comedians and clowns always got it wrong. The actor is a sober man pretending to be a drunk, a drunk is an inebriated man desperately trying to look sober. Watch the precision, the concentration of the shit-faced attempting to get across a room. It is a heroic effort. Inside that wobbling head, he is the captain of a doomed bomber struggling with the unresponsive controls, staying at his post till the last, after everyone else has evacuated—bowels, bladder, syntax—the world spins, the ground rushes up to claim him, yet still he fights for every inch of height, every ounce of propulsion, David Niven in the cockpit of his flaming Lanc talking to the ethereal, invisible, cool and admiring WAAF. Maybe he can make it to the door, to bed, to some glorious country airfield where the dog's waiting to meet him. There's a pat on the back from the CO—"Damn close-run thing"—and into the mess, barmaid already has the foaming tankard with the double stiffener on the side. She's smiling, trying to hide the tears. He leans on the bar, a pensive sigh, and slowly lifts the glass. Here's to those who didn't make it. We do good crash landings. Watch the face, the determination, the perseverance, the pursed lips, the knotted brow, the head swaying, running out of energy, feet numb on a tightrope, one stalwart leg, the other a coward. You shouldn't mock the crumpled failure of drunks but wonder instead at the repeated, determined, hopeless bravery of so many postponed calamities mentioned only in imaginary slurred dispatches.

I CAN'T REMEMBER what our bedroom looked like. The flat was the basement of a terraced house in Wandsworth. Bennerley Road. I can't remember the number. A living room, a bedroom, a bathroom, a kitchen and the small garden we shared with Chris, the landlord upstairs. I remember the kitchen. Small like a galley with a back door onto the ignored garden, a no-man's-land of dead pheasants, sodden barbecue and more dog shit. There was a Welsh dresser, an oven, a sink, a table pushed up against a wall. I can't remember the chairs or if there was anything on the walls or the tea towels—which is odd, you can always remember tea towels. Were they white or colored? Did they have ironic pictures on them of seaside towns and recipes for regional specialties? There was a radio and the radio was always on. Always. No exception. On in every room. I couldn't sleep without a radio. The BBC World Service at night. "Lilliburlero" played by the RAF band. The

Shipping Forecast. *London Calling*. Then Radio 4 would start in the dawn—*Farming Today*, beef prices, wheat yields. After a fitful night of African politicians, the radio was like a parent. I was brought up by the Home Service. It was moral and dependable and it had a plan. It knew where it would be at any given hour. It had rules. I understand why Home Service listeners get so upset when schedules change. I get upset. Everything else in life is random and collapsing, fateful and a disappointment, but the radio is a fixed point. Something you can't grasp, but you can hold on to.

The bedroom had a window, there must have been a wardrobe, a chest of drawers, a mirror somewhere, something on the walls—what color were the walls? The carpet was green— there was a green carpet . . . the color of algae, the damp green of penicillin. I remember how it smelled, it was like a living thing, the pelt of something that hid terrified and shivering under the furniture in basements. The bed was big, with an ornate headboard carved with herms or caryatids, cherubs, griffins, basilisks, cockatrices, black oak nightmares. It was a Cromwellian bed for morbid lingering, a laying-out bed, already half a coffin. I don't remember the counterpane or the blankets, quilts or pillows, I remember how it smelled. It smelled like it had been having rough, nonconsensual sex with the carpet, the sour-sweet sweat of the sorry mold-green abused carpet. You can't get any lower than a basement carpet.

It was in the bed that the DTs came. One morning I woke up. Waking up is not a given for a drunk. It's not a simple transition. It's not how you wake up, like turning the key in the ignition—a couple of coughs and you're ticking over in neutral. A drunk's awakening has layers and protocols. There is a great deal of spare and lonely emotion that has to be acknowledged, folded up and buried between sleep and consciousness. There is the panic of unresolved fright left over from the badlands of sleep. Every drunk has a procedure for getting things locked back and away in their crypts and cages. I was gingerly negotiating the painful roundup when there, just there, right there on the ceiling, there were spiders. Spiders hanging on to the ceiling. They were off the reservation, out of the box. They weren't the shades of night, they were huge, the size of soup plates, heavy as guilt. They scuttled. No, spiders don't scuttle, they move with a horrible purpose. Spiders octorate. They are always on a mission. These ones octorated across the ceiling from behind the wardrobe that may or may not have been there. They were hairy. And I knew they were going to fall on my face. They were bigger than my head. Simultaneously I also knew empirically, practically, that spiders bigger than your head were not indigenous to Wandsworth. So, sensibly, like a five-year-old, I closed my eyes tight and waited for them to go away or get back inside wherever it was monstrous impossible creatures lived.

I've had a lot of hallucinations in my time, from acid before it was moderated and pasteurized into an easy psychotropic disco drug, when an LSD workout lasted a day and came with added flashbacks that would slap your retina a month later. We would advise each other not to drop tabs alone, a trip was a dangerous saga. I'd seen the wallpaper turn into an earth

mother's pulsating womb. I'd seen vacuum cleaners become
Jack's beanstalk, I'd stared into a sugar bowl for five hours,
downloading the secrets of kinetic sweet energy. I'd watched
the traffic on Tottenham Court Road turn into a carousel, I
knew all about hallucination. And these spiders weren't hallucination. I got out of bed in a cold panic of twisted sheets
and palsied limbs. The spiders came after me. The brilliance of
delirium is that it happens only when you're sober. You can't
blame it on the port or the absinthe. I was straight-up, single-
visioned, unslurred, unprotected and utterly unprepared. The
trick, the cure, the prophylactic, is to get drunk again as
quickly as possible. I understood this instinctively. But then,
the answer to most things was to get drunk or drunker. I
sucked a whiskey bottle in a corner, not daring to look up. It
wasn't the first time I'd drunk to make things go away, but it
was the only time it worked.

A DOCTOR TELLS ME that the rarity of DTs in modern drunks
is because alcoholics get help—or at least medication—much
earlier these days. They are given Valium, a really simple cure
for the horrors. Not actually a cure of course, just a muzzle. It
pulls the curtains and keeps the spiders on the reservation. Before Valium, DTs were a favorite image for filmmakers. Billy
Wilder's *The Lost Weekend* has a rubber bat that eats an imaginary rat; there is something crawly in Blake Edwards's *Days of
Wine and Roses*. Charles Laughton, in David Lean's *Hobson's
Choice*, gets a giant rat at the end of his bed, and then there's

Harvey, the urban rabbit in James Stewart's hallucination. I think that's the only case of a hallucination from a chronic illness getting its name up in lights—and not just imaginary ones.

Drunks' horror visions are almost always animals. A small medieval menagerie of the repellent and fearful; things that share our homes, under the floorboards, in the rafters. They can come with a tactile hallucination technically known as "formication." You feel things crawling all over you, 3-D sense-surround hallucination. There was a publican in Earls Court who regularly saw Martian cockroaches landing outside his pub and would block the road with beer barrels for the safety of humans. I've only ever heard of one man who had a pleasant, though no less disturbing, hallucination. Having drunk a concoction based on bomb fuel during National Service in Malaya, he was hospitalized and woke to find a naked Malay girl sitting on the end of his bed. She gave him a medical discharge.

The shaking frenzy DTs were first described in 1813. Between 5 and 10 percent of drunks get them. Of those, 35 percent die shortly after. Surprisingly, there's very little research into the DTs, considering how much has been painstakingly discovered about Amazonian frogs and the causes of baldness. No one knows why they happen or how, but the lack of scientific interest is understandable, if not excusable. DTs are merely a curious symptom of an altogether familiar chronic condition. The Valium will smudge the visions and they make no difference to the underlying illness. They are a strange illumination that may have something to do with GABA receptors and the greed for dopamine and the serotonin of joy, the well-being chemicals that are the usual suspects implicated in addiction. Someone has suggested that the DTs may be the result of the brain's attempting to reinstate homeostasis—the body needs to maintain equilibrium, a stable internal environment to correct its psychic balance, to combat the constant intervention of alcohol. That doesn't sound plausible. The latest hypothesis, I'm told, is that DTs are something to do with scratches on the retina and the exaggerated or altered focus, which sounds even less plausible. Why is it that drunks should all find these prehistoric animal familiars, see the creatures of caves and stones, of cracks and holes? Are they perhaps found in the unvisited blackness of our mental archaeology, down beneath the conscious and the subconscious, down, down past the mysterious id into the layers of natural selection, the mille-feuille of experience pressed hard in the fossil of collective memory—this scuttling, slithering, ossified fear? There is no truth in alcohol, but it may wear away and seep down into the remembrance of things that are best left unrehydrated.

DTs were the most dramatic of my alcohol-induced symptoms, but I got them only twice. The second time, my conscious knew what was happening. I woke to find a fat toad watching me with its peculiarly evil eyes like a malevolent Eccles cake on the slime-green-algae dead raped carpet. I got out of bed and poked the phantasm with my toe. It stepped aside, slowly, theatrically. It was a real fucking toad. God knows how it had got in. It must have traveled across Wandsworth to find a sympathetic environment. Toads are notoriously choosy. I had a bedroom that was an ideal toad habitat. Getting rid of a live toad is far harder than getting rid of a hallucinatory one, but for a drunk, the method is the same. I got a bottle of whiskey and trusted that it would get bored and go away.

I picked up a pigeon in the street once. The pigeon had been hit by a car. It was alive, not noticeably damaged or bleeding, so I put it in my pocket. A pigeon will fit quite neatly into a jacket pocket. I went to the pub and forgot about it, then on to The Lindsey Club. The next day I was looking for cigarettes and there was the pigeon—head cocked, round-eyed, blinking. I was surprised to find it in the coat dropped on the floor, incubating five Gitanes.

Pockets were a constant source of surprise. A lamb chop, a votive candle, earrings, lockless keys, a photograph of an old man with a mustache and a harmonium, scribbled phone numbers, addresses and cards, notes written on paper ripped from books and menus—"Don't ring the bell," "This is the last time," "You owe me five" crossed out, "fifteen" crossed out, "twenty"—the bone of an ice lolly with a strawberry dampness. Morning pockets were like tiny crime scenes. And then there was the pigeon. I put it on the bed with the dog. They stared at each other. I threw a slice of bread on the bed, the dog ate it. I put another under the pillow, expecting the pigeon to find it. The pigeon lived on the bed for days—I don't know, maybe weeks. The dog on one side, the pigeon on the other, me in the middle. It didn't move much, just crapped a little. It didn't seem to get any better or any worse, never complained or asked for anything. A girl came over—this was after Cressida left—and complained about having to sleep with a pigeon. I said I'd sleep next to the pigeon and it wouldn't touch her—it wasn't that sort of pigeon. It wasn't carrying anything, it had a right to be there. We all had to sleep somewhere. There was something biblical about the pigeon, like Noah's flung prayer of hope against hope. When everyone else is dead because of God's capricious "Fuck it, let's start again" tsunami of petulance, and the earth is a soup of floating cadavers, the dove brings back an olive twig. There is a tree, there is land, there is something to begin again. To be redeemed. The pigeon is the bearer of God's apology, although he doesn't actually ever say sorry. Omnipotent, omniscient, just not big enough to apologize. It's his covenant—never again will he give in to his own righteous rage and break everything. So the pigeon becomes the symbol of Christ. He is the newfound country, the born-again beginning. I wrung the pigeon's neck and threw it in the garden. And the thing is, I rescued it and killed it for the same reason—out of kindness.

HOW BAD DID IT GET, people ask, meaning how physically bad. Well, apart from the DTs, there was peripheral neuropathy— numbness and tingling in the extremities—and guttate psoriasis—I was covered in scabby flakes of skin and my nails bled. There was a fatty liver that just dodged cirrhosis. I had jaundice—imagining that my yellow eyes were actually stained with nicotine. The liver function returned to normal over time, the liver, as drunks will endlessly tell you, being the only organ to regenerate itself. In fact, it restores only function, not form. It isn't born again. Once crucified, it stays crucified. I got pancreatitis, which I didn't discover until I'd been sober for two decades. The doctor who told me was nervous, he fidgeted behind his desk, shuffling my results. "Look, I'm sorry," he said, "but there's no way round this, you can never, ever drink alcohol again. I know that sounds terrible, particularly for someone in your line of work." He could have meant a food critic, or just a journalist. "Really, no alcohol at all, it will be fatal. I'm awfully sorry." I let him shuffle and twitch for a moment and then pointed out that he plainly hadn't read my notes. I hadn't drunk for over twenty years. "Oh, thank God for that." His shoulders slumped, and he reached into a drawer, took out a cigarette and flicked a light. "I've been dreading having to tell you all day, really all day. Tell a food critic he can't drink, Jesus." Overcome by his relief and purloining it as my own, I forgot to ask him what pancreatitis actually was or meant. I'm still not entirely sure.

And then there was the alcoholic gastritis—a condition I developed at art school. My stomach took against alcohol, became allergic. I think that's what a different doctor said. I was throwing up a lot. I thought it was food—lunch and dinner didn't agree with me. The specialist said I should cut down on my drinking, leave out the spirits, only a little wine with meals, you know. I did know, but that wasn't an option. Doctors have an uneven and emotional relationship with alcohol advice. For most of them, it's not medical, it's personal. So I learned to live with the vomiting and gave up eating instead. The worst was the morning. I'd slump onto the bathroom floor and heave and heave bitter teaspoons of yellow bile until my ribs ached like I'd been beaten up, and I'd burst the blood vessels in my forehead and in my yellow eyeballs—it was painful and foul and humiliating. It became my morning routine, like running a bath that would invariably grow cold without my ever stepping into it, and making a bone-china cup of Earl Grey tea that I would never drink. I always made sure I had scented soap and loose-leaf tea. If I couldn't drink like a gentleman, then at least I could greet the day like a retired governess.

When people, sensible, drink-aware people, ask how bad it was—What is the difference between terminal velocity of alcoholism and amateur dabbling, simply being bibulous? When does a boozer, a quaffer, a bon viveur, a trencherman, become an incapable drunk?—they always want a figure, they want volume, they want a fixed point, a map reference, and I don't really have any idea. I don't know how much I drank. I suppose it was probably a bottle of Scotch, half a dozen cans of Special Brew and then five or six or twelve pints in the pub . . . I don't know. I didn't want to be drunk all the time. I just didn't want to be sober ever. After the first slug of whiskey or flat Special Brew had been negotiated, winched up to the mouth using a towel as a sort of sling pulley so as not to break my teeth, the shakes would subside, like settling tectonic plates, and I'd have a sweaty bitter moment to consider the day and offer a morning prayer. I've always been doubtingly religious, faintly irresolutely spiritual with a cowardly fawning low Christianity. I'd ask God to send me an incurable illness, a fatal condition. Sometimes I'd include the loss of a limb or the addition of a prosthetic; I'd ask for swellings and lumps, wasting and sloughing, a cough and the expressionism of expectorant blood. Perhaps speaking tubes and head wands, alphabet boards, crutches, a wheel-chair, dialysis, cardiac paddles, emergency boxes of needles and ampoules, oxygen tanks. I prayed humbly and sincerely and without regret for an irrevocable death sentence. I didn't ask from rage or irony, not to shake a fist at the uncaring heav-ens, but with honest sincerity. I prayed like a self-mortifying hermit for terminal cancer. It seemed to be the only thing that would make sense of the pathetic ashes of my life, in all its grubby foul-breathed motiveless hopelessness. A tumor would give it purpose, would be the key, the excuse for the self-pity, the Rosetta Stone that would render the random hieroglyphs of incomprehensible waste a coherent story. I suppose, if you want to place a milestone—that was how bad it got. Of course, it was only in retrospect that I realized my prayer had been answered by a benevolent loving god—I was asking for the one thing I already had—alcoholism is an incurable condition that leads to the death of almost all who contract it. Anything that's bad enough to make Huntington's chorea look like an escape is pretty damn terminal. Of course, if I couldn't have a biblical illness, then I'd have to make do with whatever shards of misery were on hand. I could make the most of a broken marriage.

THE MORNING AFTER CRESSIDA LEFT, there was a man on a scooter at the door. Few miseries are as intense as the mornings of the freshly dumped. I don't want to get into a snot-spitting grief contest—there are more worthy inconsolables than the deserving lovelorn—but for sheer mortification, having your love broken over a knee, your yearning epaulets ripped off and the puppy-eyed buttons of desire cut away is right up there. The fact that no one's actually died shamefully makes it worse, and the addition of alcohol makes it much, much worse. Almost everyone has found drinking and unrequited love is not a great cocktail. There is no solace in dribbling slump drunkenness. Booze is a depressant, a close relative of anesthetic. The symptoms of getting drunk are like those of being put out for an operation—initially, fleetingly, it offers a lift, a sense of transient joy, of confident light-headed freedom; it's a disinhibitor, it relaxes your shyness and natural reserve so you can feel socially optimistic in a room, can make a pass, tell a joke, meet a stranger. But this is just the free offer to snag a punter. Drink is, at its dark pickled heart, a sepia pessimist. It draws curtains, pulls up the counterpane. It smothers and softens and smooths. The bliss of drink is that it's a small death. The difference between you and us, you civilian amateur hobbyist drinkers and us professional, committed indentured alcoholics, is that you drink for the lightness, we drink for the darkness. You want to feel good, we want to stop feeling so bad. All addictions become not about nirvana, but about maintenance. Not reaching for the stars but fixing the roof.

The doorbell. There stood Peter Carew carrying a moped helmet and wearing an old Barbour over his suit. Peter is about my age, does something in an office, and he wore the uncomfortable English face of embarrassed commiseration. "I'm sorry," he said, "I heard. Bloody business. I expect she'll be back, though. But look, no argument, I'm taking you to the country for the weekend. I was going home anyway. It'll just be you and me, it'll be fun. I've got to go to work now, but I'll pick you up this afternoon, pack a bag. Just a toothbrush, we're not dressing." At four he was back, handed me a beer, we got into the car and headed west. Cornwall or Devon, Somerset, possibly, a long journey, Friday-afternoon traffic. I expect I sniveled and Peter chatted amiably and encouragingly, the way Etonians are taught so they can lead sniveling people to wickets or out of trenches.

The house was comfortable, discreet and confident in its rightness, like dozens of similar houses folded into the English countryside like the buttons on clubbable sofas. We went for long walks and shot rabbits, and I cooked them with wine and mustard and rosemary. I did a drawing of the two of us and the rabbits, it was pale pencil and watercolor, men fading apologetically back into the paper. I met Peter's bed-bound grandmother, a lady fading back into the pillows. She seemed to be a character from Henry James. And there was a swaggering family portrait by John Singer Sargent that had been too large for the room allotted to it, so they'd cut off its bottom. An act of bravura vandalism. It was retold as an embarrassed apology with amused pride. Here is an aesthetic dichotomy—without people who think little of chopping up paintings to fit through doors, Sargent wouldn't have had anyone to render into art.

On Sunday afternoon we drove back. Peter dropped me off and gave me a bottle of Famous Grouse and wished me well.

I still remember this weekend as a supreme act of samaritan kindness. It meant, and it still means, a great deal to me. I often think of it. Retold like this it amounts to no more than a diary entry, but kindness—like comedy—is all in the timing. It was a gaping weekend of garment-rending Greek misery, whose memory has been made over as one of friendship. Peter was one of the libraryful of friends I'd married into. They were Cressida's people, these county, literary, escutcheoned rakish folk with family portraits. I liked Peter, was entranced by his easy charm, his air of fatalistic optimism. But we were utterly, utterly different. He was Eton and Oxford, cavalry and the City, one of the founders of the Dangerous Sports Club, a collection of hoorays who skied down precipitous mountains dressed in kilts and dinner jackets or sitting at grand pianos. He took to life as if it were an inheritance, which of course it is, but not for me. I was going to write that, standing on the doorstep that Friday, Peter might have been a Martian. But it was me that was the Martian . . . I had no innate, spontaneous idea of how to cheerily hum a coherent harmonious life that came with a rhythm and a tune. I looked at Peter and men like him and wondered how they did it. How did they know what to do? Say? How to be? Where did they learn the silky confidence, the certainty that everything would be all right, that they would always belong and be welcome in any room they walked into? I'd been to dinner at Peter's. Everyone drank a lot and shouted and laughed. There was, in most of Cressida's friends, a dangerous loucheness, a brilliant fatalism. It was what attracted and interested her. I expect there was a dose of it in me. We married into the golden age of dinner parties. Right at the end of the Conran chicken brick and before bean sprouts. The most popular wedding present had evolved from a silver toast rack to the stainless-steel asparagus steamer. Dinners would start with fish mousse, carrot-and-orange soup and cheese straws, and end in tears, port and infidelity. Everything in their lives ended in tears, port and infidelity. In this particular dinner party, after the beef Wellington but before the lemon sorbet palate cleanser, I went to the loo to be sick and take drugs. I looked in at Peter's bedroom and on a pissed whim took off my jeans and jersey and put on one of his bespoke suits. I left in it. Peter called the next day and laughed and said he'd swap it for something of mine. I couldn't imagine what. He strode into the gallery where I was exhibiting etchings and stole two of them off the wall. He was the sort of man who could do that. Thirty years later we are still friends. Once a year we pass in crowded rooms where he is still more at home than I am. He is pleased to see me because he's pleased to see most people. He was kind to me because he is a kind man.

A MAN, an apocryphal everyman, is traveling in a strange, imaginary land and in it he meets a stranger traveling the other way. "Excuse me, pilgrim," he says, "what are the people like in the town ahead of me?" The stranger replies with another question, "What were they like in the town you just left?" "They were kind, hospitable, generous and wise." "Well, I expect that's what you'll find they're like in the next town," answers the stranger. What a nice man, thinks the traveler. See, that's Peter, he's the traveler, I'm the stranger. I still look at him and feel like a Martian. Over the years I've method-acted some sort of learned English version of human, I can do it convincingly so that people are surprised to find that I'm not a native. But I'm not. And the town I've just come from was full of incomprehensible, anxiety-inducing social Freemasons talking in tongues, and the one I'm going to will be worse.

IF YOU'D ASKED ME what the most grotesque thing about alcoholism was, I'd have said—indeed, I did say over and over to anyone who asked—and plenty who didn't—it wasn't the physical stuff, it wasn't the sordid, humiliating death stuff . . . it was the sadness. I called it my angst. A suitable august Germanic word for a basement depression that was fathomless and occasionally erupted in gasping panic. And even when locked away, it would seep out and sour every other emotion, like bitters in milk. Alcoholic despair is a thing apart, created by the drink that is a depressant, but also the architect of all the pratfall calamities that fuel it. Alcohol is the only medication the drunk knows and trusts, a perfectly hopeless circle of angst, and it is all powered by a self-loathing that is obsessively stoked and fed. And it's that—that personally awarded, vainly accepted disgust—that makes it so hard to sympathize with drunks.

Nothing you can say or do comes close to the wreaths of guilt we lay at our own cenotaph.

There is something infuriatingly comic about drunk unhappiness, with its operatic tragic warble so out of proportion to the seedy, spivvy slapstick of its reality. From the outside it's so obvious, so easy to resolve. Just stop. Stop drinking. Stop crying. Go to the dentist. Say sorry. Get a job. Be nice.

In my adult life I have been both a bit of a failure and a bit of a success, and the difference between the two is marginal. It doesn't amount to much more than a bit more slippery guilt, a handful of ephemera, some vanity, a wider seat, a square plate, more shoes, a shorter queue and broader insincere smiles from professionals. I have also been unhappy and happy. The difference between those two is a kiss and a blow. To slip past the pragmatic balance is to go from light to dark. Kipling said we should treat success and failure just the same—and they are, almost, just the same. They dress differently, that's all. But happiness and sadness are night and day. Happiness is the only prize worth holding or giving. That's such an obvious truism. It's barely worth mentioning. Yet with the blessings of success and still with sadness, the angst followed me home like a hungry dog and whined and scratched at the door. You can't abstain from sadness, you can't renounce it or give it up a day at a time.

So there's this Buddhist monk. He lives up a canyon outside Los Angeles. He's a sort of alternative spiritual therapist.

Lots of movie people go and talk to him, and a big miserable star asks why he chooses to counsel rich famous people. "You're a monk. You own nothing. You live a life of ascetic poverty. Don't you despise folk like me with stuff and things? Aren't you fed up with listening to high-class problems?" "Oh, no," replies the monk, "I'd much rather talk to the overly rich and the super-superficially successful. You lot already know that half a million isn't going to make you happy." There is no correlation between more success and heavier happiness. And if you think you've noticed some, it's a coincidence—or wishful thinking. When you joke that money may not buy happiness but it does get you a better quality of misery, you're wrong. All misery is bankrupt. All depression paints every room gray, makes cornflakes and caviar taste the same. But then there is the dull compensation that the inverse isn't true, either. You can't increase your joy with incremental poverty or by encouraging your own incompetence.

Looking back I realize there was something that only with retrospect could be worse than misery, and you only see it over your shoulder. There is no one following you, there is very little to look back at. Alcohol is a paranoid censor erasing evidence. Blackouts are familiar to drunks and to weekend overindulgers, the curtain of forgetfulness which is often welcomed . . . What did you say? Who did you make a pass at? All thankfully erased or faded by the smudged finger of booze.

Alcoholics' blackouts can last days or weeks and they're total. I've known people who wake up in strange cities with no idea how or why. I met a man who'd spent a long weekend as a murder suspect after a girl was strangled at a party he didn't remember being at. He had no alibi—nothing. Worse was that being confronted with the possibility that he'd raped and throttled a young stranger, he couldn't in his drunken heart-of-hearts in all honesty say it was impossible. And that's a terrible thing to discover about yourself . . . without a drink, in a cell.

I once woke up with a policeman shouting at me from the bottom of my bed. What had I done? I remember that all right. I used to let Lily, my dog, out last thing. She'd come home about dawn, so I'd leave the front door open for her. In my fuddled head I was living in an imaginary prewar Lawrentian world where we all left our doors unlocked—as if Wandsworth were twinned with Candleford. The policeman had seen the door open and imagined I'd been burgled. Seeing my housekeeping solecisms, he could tell the place had been done over. I said it was the dog. I could tell he thought I was the robber—I think I was still dressed. Once, on a bender, I'd left Lily on her own locked in the house for days . . . I don't remember how many. She was so desperate for a crap she dumped a vast custard turd into a typewriter. She was a fastidious lurcher, and since she was illiterate it must have seemed like the neatest receptacle. You try getting congealing dog shit out of QWERTY keys. I couldn't face it, so I put the thing back in a box and handed it to the wife of the bloke I'd borrowed it from.

Lily came home as the policeman was asking if I could prove who I said I was. She barked, and that seemed to be enough for him. I could see he was losing interest. I got that look quite often, that "Can't be fucked" expression. I'd get it from behind glass partitions in waiting rooms, lying in dentist chairs, at reception, the "Why should I care for you if you so plainly can't be bothered to care for yourself?"

I haven't had a dream I could recount since I stopped drinking. Occasionally I'll have a sense of one, the echo of dreaming, but nothing tangible, recountable. I imagine my dream stage-manager as a man in a velvet jacket with bitten fingernails and fretting eyes, fidgeting in the wings of sleep, waiting each night to put on a performance, checking that the props are in their right places, that there's tea in the whiskey decanter, that the telephones ring. He calls, "Beginners, five minutes . . . ," the lights fade, the curtain goes up, there is the expectant hush . . . and nothing happens. Dust floats like plankton in the spotlight. He hurries to the dressing rooms, taps on doors, gently enters one after another; bulbs illuminate mirrors that reflect no one as the smell of face cream and mouthwash, costumes thrown across chairs, break-a-leg cards propped on tables with fading first-night flowers. But no one.

With a recurrent panic he runs through the theater from wardrobe to props, wigs, up to the grid—no one. And finally he goes to the prompt's little chair in the wings and grabs the dog-eared script, "Pour Me a Life" on the title page. Then nothing. He flicks through the pages—all blank. And peering out across the orchestra pit, he sees with a mixture of horror and relief that the audience has departed. Maybe there never was an audience.

So the worst thing, it turns out, is absence. Like the opposite of love being not hate but indifference. It turns out that the worst thing is not sadness, but the lack of a peg to hang any feeling or memory on. The saddest thing after all these years is not remembering. Well, who'd have thought? I miss the lost years of my twenties. All that living. All that high old emotion from that time when it's all new. The moment that was supposed to be my time, when the music was made for me, the films, the books, that great two-fisted time that is hammered out to be our time, when we set the tone, learn the moves of who we will be—the great laying down of identity. It turns out there was no film in the camera. I'd clicked away at the experience, the episodes, that would stay with me forever. But there's nothing. I don't know. I can't remember.

My dad died of Alzheimer's. I watched him retreat like Napoleon as the frozen winter of the illness buried his memories. He retreated further and further, fighting dogged but ultimately unmemorable rearguard actions over the remembrances of his life . . . from the Depression, through the war, the '60s, the Empire, Suez, postcolonialism, fascism, modernism, postmodernism. He clung to the war. The biggest thing that would happen to anyone who lived through it, the loudest memory of the century. But that too was finally reduced to rubble. I once sat on a bench in a park with him while we still knew traces of each other. The seat had a little plaque on it in memory of someone who had liked this spot. Would you like a bench in this park? I asked, leaving aside the irony of a memorial to Alzheimer's and the fact that he was not a man who spent much time on benches admiring municipal planting. "Oh no," he said, "oh no, no," emphatically, suddenly, distressed. "No.

Gwendoline Hornbeam might come and sit on me." I have no idea who Miss Hornbeam was. Hers wasn't a name that had ever met breath in any family conversation for fifty years. Here was Gwendoline, a survivor from the final redoubt of my father's memory, that fading sepia bunker where he made his last stand against the icy whiteness and the howling static. It was way back . . . back, back before the war, before a career and success and failure . . . before university and family. Somewhere at the dawn of remembrance in his Kentish childhood. There he could put the last name to a long-ago face. And after a lifetime, Gwendoline Hornbeam patiently waited, clutching a posy of some tiny spite or resentment. Once again she stood in the guttering twilight and he still couldn't bear her. It was funny and poignant. Finally, when the past had all been overrun and there was nothing but silent tundra, we would sit and eat chocolate ice cream together. The sensation, the taste, I assumed, I hoped, I trusted, meant something, took him somewhere, kindled a sense of something pleasurable. The abstract essence of a memory.

The unexamined life may not be worth living, but what's to examine if you can't remember it? Memory is the evidence of a life, and I wonder what dismembered remnants will I be left mantling like an old hawk at the end. Who will share that last synaptic spark? It wasn't just the drinking I can't remember, it is what came before it as well. Childhood, school, holidays, friends . . . all seem to be faded and incomplete, like boxes of photographs rifled in a flea market. And that is one of the reasons I'm writing this book. I really can't remember any of it.

But the act of writing, of tapping the shit-stink keys, might reveal something, jog something more, like the plaque on a bench. And that in turn will lead back to clues, to a confession, and perhaps I will be like Lord Carnarvon digging a hole in the featureless sand to discover not Tutankhamen, but my young self. Maybe just an artifact or two from which I can extrapolate a life worth examining. I'm sixty now, and wherever on the seesaw you do the actuary accounting, there is more behind me than there is to come and memories look precious. There is not enough time to make more, to fill the deficit.

A clever man said books do furnish a room—well, I have books, thousands of them. I had them then like flying buttresses up the walls, dry prose bastions and crenellations, heedless and petrified, an ossuary of books, and I loved them as you love the dead. Other men's memories. My dad taught me to love them, and loving books was the allegory we had for loving each other.

Five hundred years ago, Matthias Grünewald, Mr. Green-wood, painted an altarpiece for the Order of Saint Anthony in Isenheim. When I was young, I was entranced by it. I've never been to Isenheim, I couldn't point to it on a map, I've only ever seen the image in books. I wanted to be an artist. I was an artist. The desire is the only qualification you need to be an artist, but I also wanted to be an art student, which is harder than being an artist because someone else has to make you an art student. So I used to draw at night. I'd drink bottles of beer and draw with soft pencils on soft paper. I've always been caught on the thorns of religious art.

At the time, I had no conscious, spiritual belief. Ours was an orthodoxly atheist household. I had just a vague fugitive and ethereal neediness. The art of faith is most obviously and heroically fraught with the central dichotomy and purpose of all art—that is, to render visible what can't be seen, or perhaps to see more than is visible. At the most formal level, a painting of a landscape always represents something that no longer exists, in a place where it never existed. Religious art makes representation of an abstract. It is far more complex and meta-physically demanding than making an abstract representation of the physical, which passes the mental heavy lifting on to the viewer. The technical, emotional and intellectual conundrum of religious art is splendid, often in its failure, occasionally in its sublime transubstantiation of pigment, wood and cloth into the simulacrum of divinity. Grünewald's Crucifixion is formally familiar. Christ on the cross faces us from the center of the picture; on either side are the ever-present Mary, his mother, fainting and supported by Saint John, and, kneeling at the foot of the cross, Mary Magdalene. On the other side is John the Baptist, looking oddly insouciant, the only participant who stares straight out at us. He is pointing at the dying Christ. His stance and the finger are oddly camp, as if he were saying, "Oh, get her!" but he also holds a book that tells us what he's really saying: *"Illum oportet crescere, me autem minui"*: "He must become greater, but I must become less." It is the self-deprecating reference to the Baptist's relationship with Christ, even more so because he is already dead—he can't be at the Crucifixion, because he is already headless. With him is a sheep who looks bored at constantly being roped in as a zoomorphic metaphor. But the main event of this picture is Christ. This is the most graphically horrifying murder. The sadistic awfulness of being nailed to a post. Most crucifixions are anodyne, tasteful, even elegant representations . . . polite enough to wear in gold on your cleavage or hang above a child's bed. They are of the godly Christ, the one with the mission accomplished. He is sloughing the human to become the "great forgiver" . . . the true love. But you couldn't live easily in a room with this, with Grünewald's tortured body. This Christ is the man left behind with the agony. Too often crucifixions look like human washing hung out to dry into perfection. Chrysalises that you find on autumn twigs, a maggot that has become a butterfly. Christ, the awkward, soft halfling is become alabaster and choirs. It is the deific sacrifice, the sorry and the redemption, the gently reclining body swagged over Chippendale joinery that the church brands *Ecce homo*. But the Isenheim crucified Christ is Christ doubting, Christ forsaken, terrified, agonized. The man Christ dying by inches. His hands curled with the pain of the nails simultaneously implore the father he has never seen. It is the humanity of his death that is moving, more than the magician's trick of empty sheets and moved rock. The Christ suffers the thorns of flagellation, splinters stick in his writhing body. He is covered in sores and open lesions. The monks of the Order of Saint Anthony specifically cared for peasants who had contracted Saint Anthony's fire—an incurable condition that we now know as ergot poisoning. It comes from the mold on damp grain, which infects bread, and was endemic throughout the Middle Ages. Symptoms include running sores that led to gangrene, also hallucinations and horrors, skin crawling, shakes and itching. This Crucifixion is housed in a double-doored frame like a bank vault to hold the hideous truth of mortality. It was opened on the saint's day; poor blighted patients would have seen Christ revealed with their symptoms. Not as a savior—there was no relief, no cure—but as a fellow sufferer.

I would return again and again to this image to be moved by its horror and its beauty, but mostly by its empathy. In the moment it was being painted, Michelangelo was finishing the Sistine Chapel ceiling. This is an artistic and moral age away from that bright power, the deific superhero god zapping life into Adam. This is still the dark and superstitious old time. A year after it was completed, Martin Luther nailed his theses to the door of the Wittenberg cathedral. This is a presentiment of a Protestant Christ, and the terrible irony is that as he is the bread that will feed humanity, the body reborn in sacrament wafers, so it was the bread that poisoned and tormented the poor believing peasants. The Bread of Heaven, the salt of the earth.

Retrospectively, I realized that the scabs of my own psoriasis mimicked the sores of Saint Anthony's fire. The tingling of peripheral neuropathy, the hallucinations of the DTs, the skin crawling, were all small imitations of ergotism. What I was looking at in this Christ was the premonition of my own far more pathetic misery. So slowly I drew a portfolio of derivative and pretentious art, never really daring to go beyond the observed. I applied to art school in Falmouth. I didn't want to go to Falmouth—who does?—and they in turn didn't want me. But I did desperately want to go to Saint Martin's in London. I'd never passed an exam and I'd left my odd vegetarian Quaker hippie school without sitting any A Levels. You needed at least two to go to art school. So in the summer holiday, I took A Level art as a private candidate. I also fell for my first real girlfriend. Rebecca. She was a New Yorker, the daughter of a family friend who was staying with us in London for six months. She was twenty-six, I was just eighteen. She was terrifying. Clever. Really, really clever and sternly pretty, with a brilliantly dry deadly humor. One night, stoically, firmly, with much hilarity, she took me to her bed, like someone teaching a simple child how to cross the road. Afterward, in the dark, her face lit by the rise and fall of a glowing shared No. 6, she asked if this was my first time. No, no. Not really. Well, technically, yes. She beamed and propped herself up on one elbow. "Good. Look, there's going to be an awful lot of things you're going to want to try. You're a boy. And you've had way too long to think about all this. So relax. It's okay. We will do everything—at least once. We've got all summer." It is still the most generous and exciting thing anyone has ever said to me.

We all went to Skiathos. Rebecca, me, Mum, Dad and my little brother, Nick. When we finally got to the small house Dad had rented, it had just two rooms—one in the attic with three beds and one in the kitchen with two. It was clear to all of us that someone would be sharing with Nick. My mother took my father aside and had stern words and said to me, "You and Rebecca can have the kitchen." It was a brilliant summer. I drank a lot of ouzo, we ate on cobbled streets, made friends. There was a dairy that served yogurt every evening. The first Greek yogurt I ever tasted, with bitter local honey. I stepped on a sea urchin. Someone told us how to get rid of the damnably painful spines that break under your skin and Rebecca hobbled me up to an olive grove, stepped out of her shorts and pissed on my foot. "I said we'd try everything."

On the way to Skiathos, we stopped in Athens and went, of course, to the Acropolis and its museum. And something happened. I was walking through the great hot corridors of shattered antiquity with my father. The others were either behind or ahead of us and Dad was explaining, illuminating . . . this is what he liked doing most, talking in a museum. He was good at it, knowing just the right mix of academic and salacious. There is in all classical exhibits an overall, overwhelming sense of brokenness. Everything is a bit of something or is missing a bit. The recurring theme is not of creation but of destruction—you constantly try to repair the damage in your head, replace noses and arms, put back handles and spouts. We walked into a room and I burst into tears without warning. I was utterly overcome by sensation. There stood the blind Zeus—or perhaps he's Poseidon—one of a handful of Greek bronzes and one of the most staggeringly transcendent artifacts that is left to us. Like the Grünewald Crucifixion, it is a god as a man. This is what the Renaissance was trying to rebirth, this huge heroic vision of us made eternal. He is naked with arms outstretched, one in front to aim and balance, one behind empty-handed, his thunderbolt or trident long gone. He has lost his glass eyes, he is blind. The cruciform arms also feel in the absence of light, reaching for the edge of something, both certain and tentative; he is powerful and vulnerable, so delicately balanced on the balls of his feet. There is a name for this sudden slap of art, this falling through the rabbit hole of civilization. It's Stendhal syndrome: being overcome by beauty. They say that the guards in the Uffizi are trained to deal with collapsing Americans who have lived lives of blameless comfort in midwestern ugliness and can't compute the full beam of a Bronzino. In my case, it has happened only a brief handful of times—two of them when I was with my father, which may be no accident. The first was when he took us to Venice. I must have been about fifteen. We got lost: everybody gets lost in Venice. There was something he wanted us to see at the end of a full day of seeing plenty. And the practiced authoritative chat had turned to irritation as we complained of the heat and sore legs and being gelato-less; but we walked and we walked and suddenly we were in a square, and there it was. And I caught a ragged breath and sobbed. Verrocchio's Condottiere. Huge, totalitarian, aggressive, elegantly fascist. Not on anyone's top ten of beautiful objects—but it pulses a superhuman imperious energy. There's nothing vulnerable or lost about this man. But he is the patron of the old truth that it is better that people ask you why there is no statue to you than wonder why there is. Bartolomeo Colleoni the condottiero—literally a contractor. He was a mercenary who changed sides regularly, mostly between Venice and its rival, Milan, until the Venetians fixed him the way they fixed everything—with so much money he couldn't say no.

When we got back home, my A Level result was on the mat. I'd passed. And there was an invitation from Saint Martin's to come for an interview. Rebecca went back to New York and I to art school, where they said in an offhand way that I was welcome to join the foundation year but I really did need another exam. Would I take care of it? Yes, I said, I would. And no one ever asked for it again.

5

My first day at Saint Martin's School of Art, I walked out of a life drawing class. It was my first life drawing class. My first class. And the first time I'd sat in a room with a naked body and strangers. We all looked sideways with a glazed, pencil-sharpening, easel-adjusting insouciance as a short, stooped Greek gent in his sixties shuffled from behind a screen in a filthy dressing gown. The robe made his nakedness infinitely worse, somehow intimate, embarrassing, pathetic. It is a convention of life drawing that the models take their clothes off behind the sanctuary of a screen and then redress in a gown before appearing and removing that. There is something liturgical about it, like vestments, also something medical—an examination, a dissection. I expect it was originally to differentiate the modeling from burlesque. The act of undressing is erotic. The step from being naked to being nude. . . . from the carnal world to the classical one. Well, that's the promise. In front of us was a man with a long, sad mustache, a multitude of chins, oily, darkly stubbled, with hair grown to a fecund tilth on his Ithacan uplands. There was barely an inch of him that wasn't furry. His back was as wiry as a terrier, his chest heathery as a grouse moor, his short legs tropical. I even remember a stubby matted tail. His tight, drooping goat-udder stomach hung over a dark concertinaed penis that crouched like a bald squab in a pubic nest, perched precariously on an immense scrotum like a drop of furry creosote caught in its infinitesimal descent to his knees. Hair is the implacable, unpluckable enemy of life drawing. What we want is to render humanity divine and smooth, linear and sinewy. It is a great art joke to mock poor John Ruskin for being revolted on his wedding night by the pubic hair of his new bride, having virginally imagined that all women were as bald as classical marble. But having sat through a lot of life classes, I have a passing sympathy for him—he confused the erotic with the aesthetic, got his nude mixed up with his naked. It's easily done.

The Greek took up his position, and our drawing master, an old man with swept-back silver hair, spectacles on a chain, and an effulgent pocket handkerchief, pushed a skeleton hanging on a stand next to him. Art schools still had ossuaries of bones for memento mori. I expect the skeleton had a name. They always give the bones names. "Has anyone seen Percy or Duke?" they'd say. There are a lot of Duke skeletons. We were told to draw the man and the remains of the man so that we should be able to see how the one fitted into the other—*Ecce homo*. After twenty minutes, I realized that everything I'd confidently thought about art and drawing was a clumsy blunt smudge. I couldn't even make the body fit in the page. I failed to create one confident or even valiant line and, as always with drawing, an indecisive start simply got worse, more finger-tied. The first mark is invariably the purest—everything after that is a compromise. There is no such thing as a successful drawing. They are always qualified defeats. The Pyrrhic victory is in how close you manage to stay to the promise of the first tick. It is a brutally depressing lesson that has to be learned and accepted all at once, like a slap.

So I found myself in the late-summer sun standing on Charing Cross Road again, wondering what to do with the rest of my patently unfit-for-purpose arty-craft. And there was Mark. "Do you want a drink?" he asked. He was an original-looking man. He wore high-waisted baggy jeans, polished Dr. Martens boots, checked shirt, and denim jacket. I remember this because it was so unexceptional, so ordinary and provincial for art school, but at the same time so considered. He had a thin, pale, bony face, as if mottled parchment had been bloodlessly stretched over a high, knobbly forehead, and a nose like a broken banister. He had a thin mouth with a top lip that might have been prehensile, as if he were part okapi, all finished off with a bower of red hair that was the texture of stable straw, parted in the middle and made rigid by the application of soap. It sat on the top of his head like a jaunty, ruddy costermonger's boater; he had bright mocking gimlet eyes . . . his whole demeanor was ironic, long before irony became fashionable. Mark appeared to be wearing himself as a costume, like a Brechtian character. He would stare for long moments in shop windows or lavatory mirrors, twiddling his hair and sneering. It was vain, but it was as if he came upon his reflection as a constant surprise. I never knew what it was that Mark actually saw in himself. We walked down the street and he led me to Ward's Irish House—a cellar under Piccadilly Circus, long gone. It was a meeting place for freshly arrived Irishmen looking for work and lodgings. The barman would say, "Sure, there's a Kerry man in the corner, ask him." This was the first place I had Guinness served properly—the glasses would stand on the bar in lines waiting for their heads to settle—and they offered bacon and cabbage that was memorable. On Saint Patrick's Day, they'd sing the old songs, there would be swaying queues of slick-faced men with huge hands leaning against each other like an Oxfam bookshelf. The tiled toilet would be a melee of staggering Micks pissing up against one another's legs. It was a brilliant pub.

Mark came from Crawley but was tearfully proud of his Irish heritage. The merest mutter of an Easter rebellion or the first note of "The Black Velvet Band" would reduce him to furious-fisted drunken tears. We'd always start with the Guinness and then move on to the ironically named Black and Tan— half Guinness, half bitter. Mark was singular. We became inseparable, comrades, friends. I thought I'd come to art school for a hairy, naked Greek bloke, but actually it turned out I'd come for this odd, driven, demented, manipulative, amoral, clever and funny redhead.

There are obvious crossroads in your life—births, deaths, marriages, emigrations—but there are others, perhaps more compelling, that are hidden, that seem nothing at the time, trip wires that later you realize set off everything that came after. Everything was salted by that unconsidered decision—leaving the life drawing class, meeting Mark, going to Ward's—was a decisive moment. Like a drop of vermilion in a glass of water, it has colored everything. And now, forty years on, it's so faint that only I can see the tint.

We walked back to college and the model had gone, the easels and the donkeys stood in the empty studio, with the terrible attempts of rendering a vision of mortality still on them. They looked like sketches made by glove puppets with button eyes and thumbs for brains. There was only one halfway beautiful drawing. The figure emerged from the paper like something floating in water, tentative and ethereal; the Greek kindly—even fondly—modeled. Beside him the grinning skull . . . a *danse macabre*. Of course it was Mark's. He had the most limpid and subtle talent, elegant and skillful. The quality of his drawing was utterly unexpected. He treated it all with a bored disdain—I never saw him finish a picture; he would lose interest. Art was never a destination; art school was never the path to being an artist, it was a way out of Crawley. He dropped the pretense of art almost immediately and would nag and wheedle if I looked too intent on wasting a day working. So we roamed Soho. Sat in midday cinemas. Wandered through the openings in Cork Street, necking wine, playing pool in pubs, listening to the dissolute and bitter literary flotsam in drinking clubs. Mark had a homemade culture. In my house, we had the official received raised-brown-hardback version of culture that accepted the chronological canon of socialist middle-class taste. But Mark's was made up as he went along, from scraps and shards, random reading, an innate serial anarchy. We collected a group of fellow travelers, other art students, their mates, girlfriends, people from shops—occasionally university. The failed and the furious. In that year we became a loose band of perhaps twenty or thirty friends who would crisscross at Friday pubs in Camden and Saturday house parties in Victoria. It was my first bespoke peer group, not chosen by school or neighbors or family, not monitored or audited by grown-ups. It felt vivid and louche and giddy. The first three chords of punk were fighting the feedback and spitting in London pubs—so that's where we went to drink and buy pills. We had friends who'd play in a sort of glam-rockabilly group. Rockabilly had a now forgotten bouncy crepe-soled moment, drapes and quiffs and complicated heel and toe steps that were remarkably like Scottish country dancing. The band was called Bazooka Joe and the Rhythm Hot Shots. They played a Saint Martin's party when another feral marauding group hijacked the stage and hammered out a furious howling cacophonous set. I'd like to say we all knew that this was the opening of a Pandora's box, the start of something stinking and magnificent, but the truth is they cleared the room. We all crowded into the bar around the beer keg, dropped blues and asked who the fuck let the tossers in. Only in retrospect am I able to boast I was at the Sex Pistols' first gig.

A couple of years later Stuart, the guitarist of Bazooka Joe, called to say he'd started a new group and could I bring along some mates to hear them at the Man in the Moon on King's Road. Again I'd like to be able to tell you I felt the harmony of pop history being struck, but actually Stuart rolled around on the floor in a leather gimp mask with a zip mouth and licked my tutor's wife's nipples through her string vest and I left saying, "If he ever makes a record, I'll eat it, and anyway Adam and the Ants is a really stupid name for a group."

Mark didn't live anywhere. He sometimes got on the train home to Three Bridges and furiously smoked in the lavatory. Buying tickets for anything—paying for anything—upset his sense of himself. It was a betrayal of some personal anarcho-syndicalism. Mostly he lived on sofas. He was a bad guest. The first thing he'd do in any new house was clean out the bathroom cupboard and the bedside table of any and all prescription drugs. He pissed in any number of linen cupboards, drank and ate gluttonously and without thought. He once chewed a chunk out of someone's wedding cake the day before the ceremony. He would leave wearing your clothes, your father's clothes, occasionally your mother's clothes. He would grow attached to a feather boa or a cerise hat. But then he might also do all the washing up. He was surprisingly diligent at washing up. He was also beguiling and pyrotechnic company. I laughed a three-ring circus with Mark, had steepling conversations that built surreal worlds and populated them with phantasmagoria. I can still hear his voice rising and growing hoarse as the ideas grabbed words from his imprecise baroque vocabulary and tumbled out of his mouth into great mosaics of bawdy prophecy and poetry. But mostly he would simply sleep where he finally fell, and once comatose, he was impossible to wake— doorways, staircases, benches, the backseats of parked cars, mattresses in skips could all be home. There was a party at someone's parents' house where Mark decided to plant a tree in the living room. He came in through the French windows like a Terence Rattigan character, pulling a cherry tree in bloom that he'd spent an hour extracting with its root ball. He manhandled it onto a Turkish rug. It stood as surprised as we were. "Bring in the out!" he shouted, as if calling for the freeing of slaves or votes for women, and we pulled up every shrub and flower and shy herbaceous twig and arranged them with a manic diligence across the carpets, chairs and side tables. Pictures grew ivy, sofas became banks where the wildflowers grew, and Mark danced like a punk Puck issuing orders like a nihilist Capability Brown. At another gate-crashed party in Hampstead, he fell asleep on a spare couch in a distant bedroom and woke in the morning to the sound of a soft cough. Looking round he saw through his puffy-slitted pink eyes an intense man in spectacles sitting behind him holding a pad and a fountain pen. It was some time before the psychiatrist understood that Mark really wasn't his delusional first patient of the day.

What I loved about Mark was what I feared in myself. He had no boundaries. There was no ample sufficiency. He brooked no internal nanny. There was no small voice saying, "This will end in tears." It was always best to go on. He was— and remains—the only true existentialist I've ever known. He lived purely and solely for the life he wanted purely and solely, moment by moment. To be true to his appetites, I never saw him compromise a single selfish desire. If the Tube took too long, he would jump onto the line and walk through the tunnel to the next stop. He stole from everyone and gave away everything he had. He was utterly committed to the now. This unquestioning devotion to desire led to fights, screaming threats, goading mockery. I've seen day laborers begging him to shut up and go away so they didn't have to thump him, but they'd always have to thump him. He couldn't . . . wouldn't surrender the moment, and invariably, due to his fucked-up state, he never won, was always beaten—sometimes quite badly. I'd sit with him in Accident & Emergency ward waiting rooms while he cried and ranted and laughed and begged cigarettes to be told he couldn't smoke and then smoke anyway, doing his little dance, holding a filthy bar towel to the jagged hole in his head. He'd be patched up and argy-bargied out, and then round the corner he'd grin and produce handfuls of bottles and strips of drugs lifted from the tables of sleeping cancer patients. Mark was completely and reliably amoral. As far as I know, he never had an ambition beyond the pursuit of a memorable day. He could so easily have been a boringly good artist. He could have been any number of tedious things—clever, imaginative, personable, even charming. Along the way people would try to save him from himself, to take him on as a project. And for a moment he'd be entranced. But it always ended in betrayal and tears. Mark despised charitable good intentions as a feeble and tepid self-interest. I don't think he ever had a girlfriend. At some Chelsea party he found an empty room with a bed and engaged in a fumbling, aggravated coupling with an ugly, out-of-it junkie punk. They fornicated on top of everyone else's coats. People kept coming in to tug at their sleeves and tails, and Mark would hand out furs from under their rutting buttocks, complaining like Joe Orton's lost-luggage attendant. "You haven't come across my other glove, have you?" asked an embarrassed Sloane.

It was never going to end well. I can't remember much else about my year at Saint Martin's, but my friendship with Mark, the momentum of his hedonism, was more than I could keep up with, and I realized I was querulous where he was fearless; I worried about how to get home, would keep back a note for taxis. I was too aware of consequences, I wanted to do things, to be something else, to have stuff . . . and ultimately I wanted to fit in. I was risk-averse. In life, I realized, I would always opt for safety, and it became harder and harder to be with Mark. His consumption of everything—drink, drugs, conflict, flights of fancy—became ever more bizarre and metaphysical, out-landish. He would out–out-of-it the rest of us, he outran his friends; the infuriation with caution or compromise was fi-nally toxic, and I would avoid him. He found other, more com-mitted Berserkers to dance in the firelight with, and finally he stepped into the night umpteen floors above Los Angeles . . . or perhaps he just fell.

There is one episode—a weekend in the spring—when, late at night, drunk, wandering back to a squat, we jumped on the train at Victoria. There used to be an illuminated blue sign with a picture of the moon that promised the night train to Paris and Brussels. We took it. A fantastic rickety slow journey on rail and sea and train again. On the boat, I picked up a beautiful, dark, amused girl and we smoked joints and drank beer on the chilly salty prow and then made giggling clumsy love in an empty couchette grumbling through the creeping gray fields of Picardy. We arrived at the Gare du Nord just after dawn, kissed and said good-bye, and Mark and a couple of mates and I made our way past the street sweepers flushing the gutter to Les Halles, to drink onion soup and cognac. But what I remember most is Mark, like a character out of Dickens rewritten by Camus, dancing and exclaiming through the city and then standing in front of Théodore Géricault's *Raft of the Medusa* in a frenzy of excitement, a reverie of empathy, moved by it in a way that my measured and respectful appreciation of big pictures in gold frames could never attain. Géricault painted it when he was only seven years older than we were— madly, hubristically committed to making an emotional masterpiece. He shaved his head, lived a self-denying monastic life, built a replica of the raft, did hundreds of preparatory sketches. The sinking of the *Medusa* was a contemporary tragedy that had galvanized France with horror and fury. He interviewed survivors, who had been reduced to cannibalism, and having done all that, Géricault locked himself in a morgue with cadavers as models. When the painting was finally hung in the French Academy's annual salon, because he'd not been able to stand back from it in his small studio, he saw for the first time that the composition was wrong, the double pyramid of its structure was out of kilter; so he repainted it—there and then—surrounded by the Old Guard in their top hats and tails with their waxed mustaches and sniggering mistresses. He was driven uncompromisingly unhinged by art. The picture was greeted with gasps, a frenzy of adoration and disgust. It remains the archetypal work of Romanticism, the tangled heroic rags of bodies, the lost, the dying. I had never seen it in the flesh before this trip . . . it is really monumentally huge . . . overwhelming; it carries two stories—the *Medusa*'s and Géricault's. In reproductions in books, you don't notice, you can't see, the *Argos*, the little ship on the horizon that will rescue the survivors. They are to be saved. It changes everything. Seen small on a page, it is a painting of hopeless despair. In life, in larger than life, it is the triumph of life—and Géricault. He would live only another five years; he died of consumption at thirty-two.

On the way back to London, the train was packed. We sat in the corridor with a handful of Bulgarians coming to find work, their pockets full of bottles of plum brandy. A year later a man I knew at college, a dull man, introduced me to his new girlfriend. It was the girl from the boat. We smiled and shook hands.

Recently I was remembering all this, talking to one of that loose group of friends—Jo, who compromised on her life less than most and is now a trance-dance DJ and sells cotton dresses on the beach in Goa. I was trying to remember what happened to all the rest, all those leery Spetsnaz punks. She remembers these things and ran through the litany of names with police-style descriptions: ". . . You know, the one with the wrong name and the laugh like a flat battery . . . The redhead Mohican whose friend caught his cock in one of his millions of zips and had to call the fire brigade and they said it was too small for them to send an engine—well, that was an overdose," and ". . . AIDS." Then ". . . suicide . . . hepatitis . . . AIDS . . . suicide . . . fell under a bus . . . sclerosis . . . psychosis . . . disappeared . . ." It was a higher attrition rate than a Pals battalion on the Somme.

At the end of the year, Saint Martin's decided they had no more use for me. I sat through a grisly interview for the painting school chaired by Freddie Gore, RA (Royal Academician), the third-rate son of the second-rate Spencer Gore. He looked at my sparse and halfhearted portfolio and asked who my favorite painters were—a question that still makes my mind go blank. I plucked Cézanne. "Name all the Cézannes in public collections in London," he snapped. I stumbled through those I could remember. "Oh really, really?" he harrumphed, like a prefect who's caught a malingerer cheating. "How can you possibly say you love Cézanne when you don't even know the best painting in London, the wonderful self-portrait in the Courtauld." There isn't a self-portrait in the Courtauld, I replied. I think the picture you mean is a copy of a self-portrait, by Roger Fry. Gore blinked and pursed his lips. Another member of the board whispered, "I think he's right, Freddie," and he shuffled his paper and said, "We'll let you know." We all already knew. I offer this story not to show off my cleverness but to underline it. This wasn't the first time I'd suffered from being too clever by half. A peculiarly English defect, and of my many faults the one I have the most difficulty giving up, or even amending, is priggishness. Even as I am being a prig, I can feel a contrary warmth. I realize with a blush that in life's revels I am cast always to be a Malvolio, however much I'd like to imagine myself as Toby Belch,

Aguecheek or Feste. (Incidentally, the character of Malvolio is said to have been based on a Yorkshire magistrate, an MP, Sir Thomas Posthumous Hoby, an austere Low Churchman who sued his neighbors in the Star Chamber for coming into his house, playing cards, drinking, carousing, threatening to ravish his wife and ridiculing Puritans. He won his case but also the odium of his peers and a sort of immortality in *Twelfth Night*. You can see a carved and painted memorial to Sir Thomas in the parish church at Bisham . . . and while you snigger, I am perfectly aware that this is an inexorably priggish aside. But I simply can't help myself.)

I got a job in a dirty bookshop on Archer Street in Soho. Public displays of sex were still coy and euphemistic. Soho was poxed with strip clubs and clip joints known most tautologically as "gentlemen's clubs." They served nonalcoholic champagne in tiny basements where chubby, pinch-faced girls would palely bulge out of suspenders and totter around juggling their sagging tasseled tits for the disappointment of drunk tourists and questing public schoolboys. This was still the world of the Maltese Mafia, which was said to run all the vice in Soho. You could still get razored there—razor crimes sound so quaintly Victorian. Prostitutes would ask if you wanted company or had "got the time, dearie?" They sat behind lamps draped with red chiffon scarves in tiny rooms that smelled of Floris talc, carbolic, sweat-sour mattresses and damp towels. The sex business was a make-do, hand-cranked cottage industry. A vestige of the '50s. Its austerity and aesthetic were hopelessly, marvelously out of touch with the moment. The look of the girls, the music they jigged to, the clothes they wore, the men who pimped them, the customers who lusted over them, were all remnants of a faded, shabby, keyhole-frotting Britain. A Britain that in every other facet of life was dead and gone, built over by pop music, fashion, Terence Conran, Sunday papers, Martin Amis, garlic and avocados and the contraceptive pill. Soho's sex industry was so conservative, nostalgic and prim it should have been looked after by the National Trust. It was more snobbish, timid and badly dressed than the Church of England. A business that was defined not by what it could do, but by what it couldn't do—the restrictions were what made it so compelling. It was not even the fig leaf of pretense that the sex business was anything more than delayed disappointment; it wasn't coitus interruptus, it was interruptus coitus. Always a con, a promise that fronted a lie, and in a fundamental lie, probably much closer to being a home truth about most sex lives.

I was introduced to my job by an old and devout Jewish man whose family business was the manufacture, importation and distribution of barely titillating magazines for the damnation of the goyim. He took no pleasure or pride in his profession, he began by asking me what a young man like me wanted to work in a shop like this for. By "young man like me," he meant someone who spoke with a boarding school accent. It didn't take long to master the rudiments of the job. The small, dark shop was guarded by the traditional plastic-strip curtains that were supposed to both ease entry and prevent identification of those entering. Inside, there were tables and shelves with piles of magazines, most sealed in plastic bags. Their covers promised

Swedish nymphos hard at it and boarding school tarts who couldn't get enough man. There would be pictures of women with elaborately backcombed and lacquered hair and heavy, ungainly breasts. The magazines also tended toward unlikely jewelry—a string of pearls, a tiara—implying class, luxury sluttishness. Stomachs were sucked in, backs arched, pale and soft. This is sex before gyms or diets or fake tans. The punters would spend a long time looking at these bags, trying to imagine their content. Sometimes they'd hold them as if trying to weigh the volume of breast and buttock inside. Then they'd come to the till and purchase one, which I would put in another bag, and I'd hand them their change without looking at them. Eye contact was strictly forbidden in the dirty-mag business. We weren't selling sincerity or building customer relations; you weren't asked to come again soon. I did have to surreptitiously watch for shoplifters. The ethics of stealing wank mags is a moot point. Is it a double negative? Do two immoralities make a morality? I had to make sure that no one opened the packets in the shop—they mustn't see what it was they were buying, because that would spoil the whole business model and the fun of anticipation, which very soon would turn out to be the only fun on offer. The rules about what constituted pornography were absurd and piecemeal and exacting, constructed by people who were embarrassed, confused and fascinated by the whole business of having to make up rules for bum holes and fluids and depilation. You could imagine the committees of seriously committed, socially conscientious censors sitting in offices being presented with reams of tepid filth by sour-faced secretaries holding their noses, forcing themselves to make decisions and have opinions about splayed labia, pierced foreskins and wheelchair access (there is a well-subscribed proclivity for sex with paraplegics and amputees). Their decisions and opinions made mindful of inquisitive children, the weak-minded, the lonely, the imbecilic, obsessive masturbators, the sexually numbed and bereft and those avoiding eye contact. They decided that this or that particular image or exotic suburban discomfort in *Slave Market Gang-Bang* number three overstepped some glistening scribbling mark. For instance, you weren't allowed to show erect penises. There was the famous Mull of Kintyre concordat, like the Geneva Conventions. An agreed formula for erections. Nothing elevated higher than the knobbly holiday promontory hanging off the groin of Scotland was allowed to be sold. We couldn't show or encourage perversion or aberrant behavior; role play was bearable, as long as it wasn't too Brechtian and didn't look like you meant it. Rape fantasies were generally acceptable—apparently being neither perverted nor aberrant. Vaginas were photographed with an intense and furious intimacy. Their examination was forensic and interrogatory. Labia were pulled apart, lenses elbowed through things, investigative fingers were plunged . . . searching for what? Contraband? The hidden good stuff? It was as if the vagina itself couldn't possibly be all there was, there must be something more, something else up there. Some secret members-only club, a better appointed first-class snug, because all the fucking fuss, all the fucking morality and fucking prudery and fucking guilt and weeping, yearning, really couldn't fucking have been all about this . . . this fucked-ragged hole. It was as embarrassed as anyone.

Occasionally someone would open a packet, peel back and splay its pages in front of everybody in the shop and shout, "Is this all? Is this what I paid five pounds for?" The best customers were the prostitutes who'd come in to restock their waiting rooms. They were loud and drugged and drunk and cackled and gave me cigarettes or took my cigarettes, and were repellent and beguiling in equal measure. The shop stayed open till eleven at night, and Soho at night, after the office drinkers had wandered to the Tube, was a place of solitary, lonely men staving off the demons in the shadows, aching for companionship, angry at what life had withheld from them. I had one sadly regular customer. He never bought anything—he didn't have any money—he was a sliver of a man, gimlet-eyed with a charming smile. I'd share my supper and smokes with him. He was lonely like everyone else, but his loneliness seemed somehow deeper, more pathetic. His story was that he'd left the army with shellshock and lived on the streets as a drunk beggar, then been rescued by a Christian woman whom he always referred to as "Mrs. Sinclair." Mrs. Sinclair was a widow who had been left a comfortable fortune. "She was an angel of mercy for me," he said. "I can never, ever repay her for what she did." And his eyes would fill with tears. "She took me to a restaurant with tablecloths and everything. I ate a steak. It was called something in French and I drank water from a bottle, because she said I shouldn't drink alcohol anymore, and I've never drunk since. She found me lodgings and I got a job as a porter in a block of flats that she lived in up in Maida Vale. She was the most wonderful woman I ever met. I owe her every-thing . . . everything. She's a very religious lady, Mrs. Sinclair, and you know, Adrian, I have a very large unnaturally long penis. It's the least I can do for her."

Round the corner on Great Windmill Street was The Nosh Bar, where you could get kosher salt beef on rye bread with sour pickles and lemon tea and Middle European cheesecake, served by incredibly rude old men with grudging demeanors and immaculately Brilliantined hair. There were pictures of boxers and old fight posters on the walls, which were streaked and nicotine-stained. They remembered Solomon's Gym round the corner, where battalions of Jewish pugs had jabbed and dodged their way out of the Diaspora. Kosher nosh has all but vanished from London now, as refugees have found better things to do than make sandwiches for porn peddlers, prosti-tutes, toothless cornermen and the hard-faced, long-legged chorus girls from the Windmill Theatre. My bookshop also sold real books, but only dirty ones. Half-crown eighty-page titillators with terrible syncopated descriptions of thrusting nipples, randy manhoods and spent seed. We also stocked any-thing that had at one time been banned, censored or railed against by Malcolm Muggeridge from the pulpit at the *Sunday Express.* So along with *Secrets of Saint Agatha's Nymphos,* I read *The City and the Pillar,* Gore Vidal's novel about a boy coming to terms with gayness. It was controversial in 1948. The fact that it was still being sold as a rude book in a sex shop in the '70s told you more about Soho and the sex business than about the book. I also read *Last Exit to Brooklyn* by Hubert Selby, Jr.—a tough, brutal, ugly book that is really a series of cohabiting short stories about the life of the poor in New York in the '40s and '50s. It was . . . it is, transcendently brilliant. One of those books that changes everything else you read afterward, and it caught me at exactly the right moment, in the right place—rudderless, drunk, speedy, sitting in a shitty seedy sad sex shop in Soho with no plan, no expectations. It had been prosecuted for obscenity. First privately by a Tory MP, Sir Cyril Black, an extreme Baptist. There was a public prosecution in Marylebone, where Robert Maxwell spoke for the prosecution and Anthony Burgess and Frank Kermode for the defense. The judge insisted on an all-male jury because the book would be too distressing for women. The chaps, obligingly and manfully, found it guilty of obscenity, which was overturned by a man in a wig on appeal. It's difficult now to imagine, but I have lived through a time when judges could stipulate single-gender juries for the protection of the fainter (*sic*) sex. Cyril Black's grandson Andrew Black set up Betfair, the online gambling site, which may have sent the bigoted old censorious Baptist spinning in his grave like a slot machine.

Selby wrote *Last Exit* because he had pulmonary disease and couldn't work. He said, "I know the alphabet. Maybe I could be a writer," which is the punk instruction for literature. He did. Selby was a drunk and a junkie and he got clean and he got sober and he stayed that way. Did it for the rest of his life, even refusing morphine in his final illness. He was one of us who made it all the way to the end. He said that *The New*

York Times wouldn't review any of his books, but they'd publish his obituary. And they did.

I loved Soho. Its louche, weary, dog-eared smutty brilliance. The pubs full of bitter, drunk nearly-wases—men with ancient tweed jackets that were too lazy to leave them and yellow fingers, who smelled of Gitanes and whiskey at ten in the morning. Men with everything behind them, for whom a lacerating envy and a general livid malevolence were the sour elixir of life. They had once all been promising novelists championed by Hugh MacDiarmid or John Braine, they'd come down from the grit of the north to take London by the throat and now chased reviewing jobs for *New Statesman* (known as "The Staggers" because of its constant funding crises) or as freelance subs on late-night shifts on the tabloids. Men who'd once had poems published in *Encounter* and been included in anthologies of *New Voices from a Young Albion*. The Soho pubs— The Coach, The French, The Intrepid Fox, The Blue Posts, Muriel's—were all blistered with them. They made failure a marvelous lifelong calling, polished their doggerel stories of disappointment till they shone with a lacerating brilliance; and the women were perched at bars like ailing marabou storks, cadging gins and pulling the filters off Benson & Hedges . . . fillies who had once played opposite Roger Livesey, who'd been the mistresses of plutocrats and publishers, who had been whisked off to Brighton in bull-nosed Morrises. Women who had been free and vaunted and famous for their beauty and their wit and their fun, who had run from the fearful postwar probity of suburban housewifery to be modern and liberated, who had handed over their youth and their enthusiasm, their talent and their bodies to difficult men as if they were mere bagatelles. Men who'd lied slicker than they, and moved on, faster than they, and had left them here, washed up in Soho. The great anecdotal reef of lies that had been sucked dry, killed by promises and the dreadful amusing cruelty of drunken bravery. I was desperate to be part of it all. But you have to try something to fail. Doing nothing—reading in a dirty bookshop—isn't something you can fail at. Soho was the pantheon of cataclysmic collapse, and I hadn't earned my place in it yet. So I decided to go back to art school and sent my portfolio to the Slade. Much to my—and everyone else's—surprise, I got an interview. This time there was no board, just Professor Gowing, the newly appointed head of the school.

Lawrence was a singular man, an art historian. He had a distinctly patrician air about him, although he was a draper's son and largely self-educated. He had been at best a dull painter of the Euston Road School, producing mundane but closely observed life studies and studiously unflattering portraits and some landscapes that made everything look like a bomb site. I'm told he wrote a brilliant book on Vermeer, but far and away his most striking attribute was his prodigious, gorgeous ugliness. He was histrionically hideous. Mythologically misshapen, large and uncoordinated. He resembled an evil fairy's unsuccessful attempt to turn a gargoyle into a frog. He also had a wholly inappropriate penchant for wearing leather, and if that were not enough, he boasted the most severe and overwhelming stammer I've ever heard. I suffered a stutter as a child, I know how embarrassing and self-conscious it makes you. Gowing's was like a comic seizure. The word or syllable would jam like a bone in the back of his throat. He'd contort and shake his head trying to dislodge it, glottal gasps and exclamations would emerge, and then silence—just the terrible, fat, pendulous head straining like a choking mastiff. His cheeks wobbling, the long puce and shiny bottom lip hanging, the numerous chins shaking, he would cup his hand under his strange jaw as his eyes blinked and bulged and long streamers of viscous spit would be propelled from his silently ululating mouth to be deftly caught and replaced in the frothing maw. Finally, in an explosion of saliva and pent-up breath, the word would be expelled like a gobbet of fat. Talking, for Gowing, was a continuous series of self-administered Heimlich maneuvers, yet this was a man who'd chosen to surround himself with the greatest evocations of beauty, elegance and eloquence and to make his life's work explaining them. He could have hidden away in the storeroom of the draper's shop; instead, supremely unaware or unconcerned by his Caliban-like entrance to every room, he was an inspired and inspiring lecturer whose basic art history course that we all had to do was one of the most invigorating, humane views of the marathon of Western art that I've ever heard. He had a particularly clear eye about the nature and the process of being an artist. The collision of the vision and the imagination with the real and the practical and the dexterous. The difficult and frustrating conjunction of hand and eye. Though his lectures could go on a long time, and he did quite often dribble into the slide carousel, making the

Virgin's face buckle and squirm like an early disco effect, he was a quite remarkable man, both for what he saw and understood and for what he chose not to see or comprehend.

We had a brief chat about drawing and he said, "Well, Adrian, most of this is terribly derivative and underworked. I see you're lazy and facile, so, all in all, we've decided to phu-phu-poh-arrarr-ttttt!!!!!! . . . t-TAKE YOU on and teach you something."

Art schools had just gone from offering a diploma in art and design to giving out degrees. The Slade, being part of University College, came under the national stipulation that to sit any BA course, a student must have achieved at least two A Levels, which of course I hadn't. But colleges that taught art or performance could claim a dispensation to set aside the academic requirement in cases of exceptional talent, which was how Gowing got me into the Slade. I'm eternally grateful to him and I continue to be a disappointment . . . stubbornly, remedially lazy and facile.

6

The Slade set out its studios rather like an old haberdasher's, each room favoring a particular sort of work. There were the dungaree-and-roll-up abstractors, the symbolically empty studio for performance and conceptual, the life drawing rooms, the sculptors and the old life room with its crow's-nest balcony—built so that the professor could make sure students weren't abusing the models—which was used as the studio of imaginative but observed art . . . that particular English vision that is prosaic and lyrical, a perceived, quiet, rational mysticism that really was the Slade's historic forte. The place was choked with the ghosts of Bloomsbury painters: Augustus and Gwen John, Mark Gertler, Dora Carrington, Duncan Grant; the war painters Paul Nash, Christopher Nevinson, Wyndham Lewis, David Bomberg, the Spencers—Stanley and Gilbert—and my totemic favorite, my guardian ghost, Isaac Rosenberg, the East End peddler's son who came to the Slade and painted a brilliant self-portrait. He looks sideways out of the canvas, wearing one of his dad's good suits with a wide-brimmed hat. It is a picture that manages to be both self-revelatory and questioning. It comes to us with the dabbed insight into the new century—culture, identity, vulnerability, wisdom, humor, youth and belief. It is far greater than any of the other pictures he ever made. Occasionally there are artists who have only one image in them, they repeat it like an infuriating chorus. Rosenberg did his just the once. It was as if he were painting a posthumous cover for his best work. He found his most profound images in poetry and the trenches, where he was killed. I've always felt a kinship with him based on no more than this picture. Our backgrounds and lives couldn't be more different, but I also moved from the linear to the literal, and he died on April Fool's Day, the day I stopped drinking:

Blind fingers loose an iron cloud
To rain immortal darkness
On strong eyes.

The roll call of the Slade's shades hung heavily in the charcoal air: Michael Andrews, Richard Hamilton, Patrick Heron, Osbert Lancaster, Oliver Messel, Eduardo Paolozzi, Paula Rego, Matthew Smith, Edward Wadsworth, Craigie Aitchison, Don Bachardy, G. K. Chesterton, Robert Medley, Eileen Agar, Rex Whistler, both Gores (Freddie and Spencer) and the eminent recorder of unsuccessfully repressed homosexual scouting, Henry Scott Tuke. They are such a diverse arty list, but at the same time there is something terribly familiar about them, variations on a theme. They're redolent of a particular Englishness—solitary, crafty, eccentric, depressive, intensely observant, equivocal, better at retrospect than premonition, doubting, maudlin, deeply, speechlessly sensitive to the rhythm of things, the entropy of passion, love and the windlass of seasons and hope and harvest. It is a collection that forever looks out of a library window on a Sunday afternoon in September with the smell of burning leaves, gravy and self-abuse. It is literal and literary; immortal darkness on strong eyes.

I once interviewed a very short-tempered Howard Hodgkin, and he erupted with a paean to the inability of the English to see, or make, good artists. The fault, the insurmountable fault, was apparently Shakespeare's . . . him and the Book of Common Prayer . . . and the dictionary. It was the English language itself, so voluminous, logorrheic, sinewy, subtle, pugnacious and duplicitous (my words, not his). Only English could describe the gallimaufry and the cornucopia of itself. The English, he said, were so spoiled and awed and besotted with writing that they saw the plastic arts as secondary, a charming craft or self-expression. The best those not blessed by the word could hope for would be to become licensed illustrators of poetic insight. It was typical that the Pre-Raphaelites, controllers of such technical mastery, such explicit vision, should also attach stanzas of verses to their pictures—the quotes of their betters, the approbation of words like the comments of teachers. The English look for stories in art, not feelings.

I've just seen Hodgkin's umpteenth birthday announced in *The Times*, where he was called an "abstract painter." It made me smile. It will have made him grind what's left of his teeth. I made the mistake of asking him why he had chosen abstraction whilst all his contemporaries were figurative. He fulminated with an abstractly manufactured rage—how could I say such an asinine thing, such an unobservant, philistine thing? It was as plain as a pikestaff that he wasn't an abstract painter. "Nonfigurative?" I offered, apologetically. He was disappointed that anyone would hire a journalist manqué as dumbly unobservant as me to write about art. Where had I learned the precious little I knew on the subject, he asked. From Lawrence Gowing at the Slade, I offered. He rolled his figurative eyes. The language was conspiring against him, to mock his singular vision with intolerable labels. I think what annoyed him was that I was a turncoat who was using the pen to traduce the brush.

I moved listlessly through the studios of the Slade, not really sure where I belonged or what manner of artist I should blossom into. I avoided the life drawing rooms with their plumb lines and etiolated silences, the model arranged in an architecturally unnatural cantilever. The orthodoxy of Slade life drawing was something I knew I didn't want to acquire. I can still tell a drawing that has come from a Slade-trained hand, with its little tentative dots and crosses of measurement, the anal architectural obsession with relative space and proportion at the expense of character and emotion. Why is this girl propped like a naked plank in front of me? is a question that never sullies the artist's mechanistic reductive observation. It's not even a butcher's look at a body; there is no appetite, no intimation of blood and sinew, no muscle and warmth . . . it is very English. The style was invented by William Coldstream, the Slade professor before Gowing. Coldstream was the great painter of the Euston Road School, and everything an artist should aspire not to be—he painted in three-piece suits, wore horn-rimmed spectacles, polished his shoes, was a committee man, a clubbable man, a gentle conservative who painted a collegiate number of college principals, bishops, chairmans (*sic*) of many boards, retiring presidents, eminent alumni and the newly ennobled. Coldstream's nonjudgmental politely observed portraits must grace half the brave new white-hot streamlined executive offices of the '50s and '60s. They were the bread-and-butter work that he treated like Yorkshire pudding and gravy. He also did a lot of other paintings, beautiful, eloquent and quietly poetic landscapes and cityscapes painted through the windows of executive suites in new skyscrapers, and surprisingly erotic and knowing nudes. He painted a lot and was never what you would call fashionable, but his works rarely come up in salesroom catalogues, and when they do, they command unexpected prices. Those that have them tend to hold on to them. They speak to something in us, something quiet and amusing. They are like their creator—good in a room.

Coldstream affected none of the glamboyance of art school teachers, the partisan, proletarian clobber of a clochard's blue overalls, the earthy corduroy and canvas, stripy T-shirts and red bandannas of republican solidarity, along with the northern caps and nautical facial hair that was the predictable livery of most English artists trying to look like illustrations of themselves. His very ordinary suburban demeanor was in fact so avant-garde and provocative, so countercultural, that students adored him. When I was there, he still inhabited the Slade with *esprit d'escalier*, chatting amiably, offering self-deprecating insights and shy opinions. I once found him standing in front of a canvas I was attacking with vehement bravado. "My, my, Adrian," he said, "I'm sure this is terribly good, but I can't say I understand it. It looks awfully, awfully clever." It was only later I noticed the double awfully.

We used to drink in the same pub, the Canonbury Tavern in Islington, and he'd come over to whatever gang I was drinking with and say, "Now, I'll buy you all one pint, but I don't want to talk to any of you," and he'd go read the paper and drink whiskey at the bar. I asked him how he arrived at his method of drawing with the little measuring dots and crosses. "Well," he said, "I got to the Slade under an utterly false pretense. Tonks was the professor [an equally charismatic master of the school famous for his academic life drawing and insistence on copying from plaster casts]. I sat in the life class, which was very serious. I had no idea what to do, so I thought if I just made dots around the outline of the model and then joined them all up like a children's puzzle, well, it might turn into a nude."

I spent some time in Stuart Brisley's performance art studio. Brisley was much more the accepted vision of the '70s artist. He changed his name to his social security number and spent a week in a bath of rotten meat in Germany. I set up my easel because the studio was usually empty except for a nice girl called Kate who did feminist performances. She'd got the technicians to build her a glass box in which she would sit, wearing white trousers and menstruating. I liked Kate enormously, she was brave and strong and her piece was provocative and gentle and human—the blood not of struggle, of violence and death, but of life and love and also of shame and secrecy and lust and everything the life drawing rooms weren't. Kate confided in me that she'd got engaged to a very nice, very decent and very straight boyfriend who supported her with an uncomprehending and slightly queasy adoration. He couldn't tell his mother what she did, and she couldn't tell the sisterhood she'd done anything as bourgeoisly paternalistic as being a fiancée, so she surreptitiously removed her engagement ring when she came into college.

And then I moved down to the studio overseen by Jeffery Camp, my tutor. He was the best art teacher I've known—teaching art, as opposed to teaching drawing and painting, is empirically counterintuitive, almost an oxymoron, an impossible thing. With all the other arts, you teach style and inspiration through technique; learning to play an instrument is the way to make music. But the last hundred years of the visual arts have been dedicated to extracting the art from the craft, leaving technique aside to set creation free. So rote teaching of skills can stifle, even strangle, creation. Art schools were teaching things that we were then encouraged to forget or tear up on the way to becoming artists. Can you imagine any other discipline that suggests that—that you would learn medicine but then have to forget it to become a really good doctor? Art and craft are obviously related, and it would be a fool's errand to try to categorically untangle them. But it is a salutary aesthetic truth that too much skill will make bad art, and occasionally people with no dexterous craft at all will make exceptionally fine art; yet not everyone without skills is an artist, and those who splash about with dramatic abandon, pointedly ignoring the rules to get in touch with the essence or the muse or the feeling of creation, are, without exception, talentless glass-eyed makers of mess. But then the line between mess and art is an incredibly fine one, and it is drawn only by those who have a skill, taste, sensitivity and aesthetic understanding . . . and just because it's fine, again, that doesn't make all mess nearly art or all modern art almost rubbish.

Jeffery taught with mellifluous patience using the history of art. "Go and look at how Verrocchio makes a hand . . ." "Here see how Renoir and Raeburn treat reflected light." I found it fascinating. He had a fathomless knowledge. Not Gowing's swaggering scholarship, but a pilgrim's awe. He spent his life looking at the way others had looked at life. He explained creation with an intense mystical love. But more than anything, he just wished to be part of it, to be counted among the number. He was an RA, but more important than that, he had managed to spend his whole life doing art and therefore being an artist, and his greatest gift was in being able to pass on the quiet, intense observation and love of the seen. With Jeffery I realized that what I really loved was drawing. Traditionally, drawing is to art what singing scales is to opera—a backstage craft. Everybody who makes art draws; some, like Turner, do it obsessively and constantly; some, like Francis Bacon, rarely. And drawings aren't meant to be seen as finished things, however elaborate and skilled they are—they are always line association wanderings, thoughts on paper. The very first human art was drawing scraped with charcoal and mud or scratched with flinty nibs on rock; but sketching is relatively recent and came with the availability of cheap paper. It arrived through Venice, where rags from Constantinople were bought in bulk. Drawings became amateur, a hobby, a way into art because it is possible to learn the facile technique of drawing—like being able to play popular tunes on the piano. I loved it because its ingredients are cheap and disposable and don't intimidate. It's like wanting to cook and stopping at bacon sandwiches. Drawing is immediate and equivocal, changeable and emphatic. The deepest way to learn is to copy. Copying other art is the most profound road to understanding. You look with a concentration that you couldn't muster just sitting and staring. Drawing deconstructs—twice—cerebrally and mechanically, with hand and eye. There is a symbiosis in that it is as satisfying as it is frustrating. When people say, as they do, that their children could draw like Picasso, quietly ask them to sit down and copy a Picasso. Not a complicated one, a really simple one, and in an hour they might realize what a staggering finger- and brain-defying genius Picasso actually was. I took myself to the British Museum and spent a term drawing the Elgin Marbles. It was one of the most calmly satisfying things I've ever done, bereft of point or reward, hours spent failing to master an elusive skill in the presence of stones that are the lintel and hearth of civilization. Still, whenever I visit the Marbles, I feel the echo of a sentimental camaraderie. My drawings won the oldest and cheapest of all the prizes given out at the Slade—ten quid for drawing from the antique. Two generations before me, every student would have had a portfolio of these sketches. In my year, I think I must have been the only contender. I also spent a lot of time in the print department making etchings. Again, this is an art that is made with a marvelously seductive process, the shiny copper plate, the elegant heft of the needle, the matte black of the candle smoke, examining the minute size of bubbles in the acid like a vintner peering into champagne, the burnishing and the cleaning, the silky custard of the ink, the blanket, the damp paper, the spin of the ancient press, the pinch-caught corners of rag paper lifted gently like pale flat fish; the rush of the reveal—an image created as a ticking series of craft skills that are exactly as Rembrandt or Goya knew them. Dürer could walk into a modern etching studio and go about his work without having to ask a single question. The collective, congenial club of materials and manual skills is one of the great joys of making art. The pleasure of feeling paper between finger and thumb, knowing its weight, if it's hot-pressed or not, if it's rag or wood pulp, the grades of Conté, sanguine the color of dried blood, the half pans in the watercolor box—a process invented by Mr. Newton to semiset pigment with gum arabic so that you could put a studio in your pocket. The grades and shapes of brushes, the finest taken from the tails of Russian sable that can be tied only by men with murderous fingers; the smell of turpentine and poppy oil and the dry dust of pastels and the hot hoof stew of size; the worn and familiar nature of battered, dappled, notched and smooth things in studio rooms, the pliers and knives, the handles of map chests, the fit of a thumb into a palette, the rattle of hog brushes in a jam jar, the crumbly scratch of charcoal on paper, the wet fart of the last squeeze of flake white, the dull funereal drum of well-stretched Belgian linen when it's primed, the smooth cool paste of egg tempera and the pigments with their stories, the passion of color, the lapis lazuli mined in Afghanistan and ground gently because if treated with violence it shatters to white, making a blue so expensive, so beautiful, it could only be the color of the Mother of God's robe and of heaven, the virginal white that would poison you, the pure and deadly cancerous cadmium, sublime yellow from the urine of cows fed on mangos, red from crushed beetles, imperial purple from shells traded by the Phoenicians. Pigment alone might trap and entrance you for an entire life, the kit of art is so beguiling, so completely moreish with so much flattering possibility, such falutin promise it spins out possibilities— the softness and the blackness, the subtle chiaroscuro of materials are the sirens of art, so many artistic lives have been lost, drowned in the Corryvreckan alchemy of the paint box, imagining that the medium must hold the message. In truth, it is all only dust and mud and dead things, but I can still waste a morning and a demi-fortune in an art materials shop.

I was in the studio painting when my canvas moved. I always had very good Belgian linen canvas to compensate for my very bad painting, which was like colored syrup and Marmite. I nodded my head round the easel and came eye to eye with Lucian Freud. Lucian had an intense, messianic stare, he was stroking the canvas for the passing, tactile love of it, because he couldn't resist the fingering, a quick grope. I smiled. He stared.

And that was pretty much the sum of his input into my artistic life. He taught in the studio, which meant that he would turn up twice a term in paint-stained chef's trousers and a loose cravat, looking like a buzzard who'd eaten the cook. He taught the girls. They would trail out after him for lunch at Wheeler's and not be seen again for a couple of weeks. Years later I'd see them splayed on sofas or beds in catalogues and on auction house walls. I don't know what he would have taught us, just having him there occasionally was enough. A confirmation that if ever there was a right place to be to make art, we were probably in it, but then again, just as probably, there isn't a right place to make art, and if you think you're in it you're not.

The Slade was run rather like an Oxford college . . . you had your tutor, but weren't expected to actually do anything. You could turn up when it suited you. Lectures were supposed to be interesting enough to pique attendance, and work was assessed at the end of a year. We were trusted to get on the best we could. There was a very charming old beadle called Sean who could cover for us, help lift paintings and fib about our whereabouts to creditors and young ladies. He would pop his head into the studio and say, "Adrian, are you in? I've got a Vanessa at the door—I wasn't sure if you were here . . ."

I was living with a Playboy bunny in Balham, the first girl I set up home with. We loved each other with a Narnia-like joy and a baffled incomprehension at the bizarre business of playing at grown-ups. We acquired a dog from Battersea; I thought we needed a dog. The Bunny was called Roz and was red-haired and pneumatic and very, very funny, and wore punk bondage and angora Oxfam and a look of knowing innocence like the bishop's niece caught taking a piss in the font. She'd come to the college and lie under my easel and Sean would feed her biscuits and tell her about the war. The dog, not the Bunny.

Have you ever wondered why so many junkies and drunks have dogs? You may have thought that the reason was the offer of unconditional love to the essentially and practically unlovable . . . that if your life was tripping and slipping and helter-skeltering down the waste disposal of usefulness and self-worth and everyone else who was a grown-up was telling you to pull your finger out, get a grip and accept your responsibilities and stop being such an insufferable boorish prat, a dog would be a solace. A helpmeet. An uncomplaining and, most important, nonjudgmental companion. And that is all a truth, but it's not a reason. The reason drunks and junkies and the chronically wonky have dogs is that they are the heraldic beasts of normality, the sibyls of probity. What could look more suburban and proper than a chap walking a dog? Having a dog means— or at least implies—responsibility and dependability and a pastel banality. Nothing is as ordinary as a dog. The fact that a mutt on a rope fools no one is neither here nor there, it fools the drunk. The small affectations of settled bourgeois behavior become vital to self-belief, like being able to dress right. Drunks often spend hours—days—worrying about looking believable. Most of the time at art school, I wore Dr. Martens boots, a T-shirt, an RAF flying suit, and an ancient American biker's jacket. But if I needed, I had a whole dressing-up box of suburban authority: Marylebone Cricket Club ties, pin-striped suits, brogues, hats and briefcases. The briefcase, importantly, contained Paul Klee's thin volume on drawing, Boccaccio and four cans of Special Brew. My drinking seemed expansive to most of my friends, but it wasn't exceptional. We all drank and dropped pills and smoked dope and heroin on occasion, snorted one another's coke in strangers' bathrooms. There was plenty of social camouflage for addiction and we were all art students, culture's commandos of overindulgence. But I knew, in briefly sober and lucid moments, that I had dropped the reins, I was not in control of the charabanc and I would have to stay on as well as I could. In the end it made no difference. Fidelio—the dog's faithfulness to me, and my faith in the dog-gedness of the drugs. In the end, "the drug it was that lied."

I could still work, and art was the only entry on my wish list. I drew and got good at drawing, facile, quick-fingered, but I also went to the pub. We drank and listened to bands and danced and had sex . . . I remember a lot of sex. But erotic recall is the least trustworthy of all drug memories. I walked back to my Islington digs from the Canonbury Tavern. It was only a few hundred yards, but I'd get lost and weave around the Orwell-socialist polite squares of Canonbury. Once I passed a door that was open and bright. A party was finishing. People leaving, calling. I walked in, took a can of beer. It was a little flat shared by two girls. A pretty one and a fat one, and as is in the nature of these stories, I flirted with the pretty one and ended up in bed with the fat one. I'd never slept with a fat person before. She was really, really Botero big. In proportion, vo-luminous, a beautiful smooth face with round generous eyes peering out of a harvest moon, her skin soft and smooth and as cool as a winter eiderdown. Lying with her was gentle, no edge, no bone, no muscle, just a glimmer of light, pale, unfolding body in the darkness. I held a breast with an explorer's gentle surprise, discovering that she had no discernible nipple. I sat up and stared at the luminous body and realized that I was only holding the foothills of her great rolling bosom. There was so much more to traverse, so much more corpus incognitum, a Fairydown land. I woke with the usual panic, staring at a strange ceiling. She stood in the bedroom door already in her work clothes, a neat, apologetic frock, back being a wrapped-up fat girl. She had a bone-china voice, clear and precise: "I left a cup of tea for you, I don't know if you take sugar. I've got to go to work. Pull the door, and I've left you my phone number on the table. It was nice." I didn't drink the tea and I didn't call. But perhaps a week, maybe two, later, I was lost again and recognized the door. I rang the bell and the pretty one answered, giving me the withering, sour look of a friend who's had to listen to too much. She shouted, "It's for you." The fat girl appeared, silent, weightless in her soft cotton pajamas, and gave me the shy moon smile with a beatific grace. "I'm glad it's you." I never planned to be there. I couldn't have found the house sober or in daylight, but like some bedtime story, I would turn up over the months. And then something else must have turned up. I'd probably started seeing someone or traveled, and the moonlit spell broke, and I lost the way back through the sodium night. The thing is, I must have been told her name, but I can't remember it. I don't think I ever remembered it.

After you've slept with someone, you can't ask what they're called. So I never knew. She was just "darling." My friends who never saw her nicknamed her the mattress—a bloke's witty take on the fat mistress, not kind, not fitting. I didn't miss her for years, but now, thinking back across the turn of the century, hers is the image that returns in the night, a ghostly memory of that milky body, the texture of cool white flour, the waxing voice and the waning smile.

In my last year at the Slade, I began to have doubts about art. I'd push them away, have a drink, go to a gallery. All artists have touchstone pictures. Paintings that carry a personal power beyond their art historic or aesthetic quality. You go to them in a votive way, as Druids would go to sacred trees or springs to renew and confirm that faith in the essential transcendent beauty of all art. We'd go to remember why we're part of it—this noblest of callings, to be an artist. The highest achievement open to a human. To create something profound and original is to stand above all the inventors, discoverers, organizers, multipliers, judges and sages. It is to stretch out and touch the divine. All artists see this most clearly in other people's art. One of my images is *The Vision of Saint Eustace* by Pisanello in the National Gallery. My father gave me a postcard of it when I was a child. I pinned it up beside my bed. Saint Eustace is an apocryphal second-century Roman general and a pagan who, whilst out hunting in Tivoli, near Rome, saw a deer with a crucifix between its antlers. He was transfixed and instantly converted. He went home and made his family Christian. Inevitably his life turns into a country-and-western song—it all goes wrong. He loses all his money, his slaves all die of the plague, his wife is kidnapped, his two children are taken by a wolf and a lion, but he never loses his faith; and then everything starts going right again. He gets the wife and the kids back, the money back and his position back. This is an ancient pre-Christian parable of the man tried and tested by faith. All he has to do to seal the deal of a happy pagan ending is make a sacrifice to the old gods. Oh, but of course . . . he won't. So the emperor, Hadrian, whose wall I'm named for, who gave us the Pantheon, has him and his family martyred by being roasted alive inside a bronze bull. I always thought that the person who should have been beatified after all this was his wife, Theopista, which ought to translate as "pissed off with God"—but probably doesn't. She gets baptized as a family special offer without the transforming visitation of a kitsch Christian Bambi, is kidnapped by pirates, loses her kids and finally gets it all back just for her zealot husband to righteously fuck it all up and get them cooked in a novelty oven. Eustace is revered as a saint, originally by the Eastern Church, and then in the Middle Ages in the West. He became the patron saint of hunters and, as an ironic joke, firemen. Pisanello's portrait shows the revelation as an incredibly elegant if inappropriately dressed Eustace comes upon the stag in the forest. He holds up his hand in faint surprise, his feet are pushed into the stirrups to make an emergency stop, but the horse is already placid, as is the deer, who stands impervious to the hunt, secure in the protection of his third, cruciform horn. Around them the animals of the forest are rendered serene and perfectly at peace.

In the foreground a greyhound chases a hare; each seems to be frozen in the moment as if on a merry-go-round. One of Eustace's pagan hunting dogs is caught in a halfhearted growl, more a canine sneer, really; another lasciviously sniffs the comely backside of a third. There is not a single naturalistic thought or inclination in this painting, it is a hyperreal moment of transfiguration. Everything is protected and bathed and blessed in the miracle. Nature is perfect, the unnatural, supernatural craft of God and his hand the artist immaculately observes. These aren't the mythological beasts or parable creatures, they are the Almighty's creation in all its Eden-fresh glory. Pisanello is the painter who hovers in the doorway between two rooms—the Gothic and the Renaissance. He looks with a rapt awe at the world, his characters move small and silent through the splendor, not yet the center of everything. It's not quite all about self-obsessed us. Yet. And nature is not yet a metaphor. Compare this with Giotto's wonderful fresco of Saint Francis preaching to the birds. Pisanello's nature speaks to man—with Giotto, man preaches to nature. In *Saint Eustace*, man is not yet the earthly embodiment of the divine, he still inhabits a world greater than anything we can imagine or make. Pisanello has a creative tell, an artistic tic. It's his hats. He loves an elaborate and improbable headpiece. Eustace has an artfully arranged bed on his head. His placid characters all look like great, complicated things are exploding from their craniums—maybe ectoplasm or ideas, feelings, exuberance. So I stood with the Pisanello and Saint Eustace and then I walked through the National Gallery and I knew that I wasn't destined to be a guide to Eden, that I wasn't the hand of awe and beauty and God, and still the doubts about my place in the creative world grew. I worked hard to dispel them, drew better, became more dexterous, more adept, but each stroke of craft crosses out the art. The more skillful I became, the worse I was as an artist. People who are nervous or intimidated by art look for the craft as a confirmation of quality, but artists are constantly trying to free themselves from the mechanics of making. We rely too heavily on craft to solve problems in art, and thus kill it. I ended up with something that was all potato and no meat.

As I left the Slade, I understood that I wasn't going to be an artist—not the artist I wanted to be or thought I might become. The artist that had been my only ambition since I was a child, when, at nine, I was given some oil paints and a primed board and I copied a bowl of fruit. David Sylvester, the art critic, who was working with my dad, noticed and commented on the new painting . . . and my father told him it was by me. And David took a step back and said, "Giacometti couldn't paint like that until he was twelve." The realization that I wasn't going to be a great artist was a profound sadness. Jeffery, my tutor, dolefully said that he was a great believer in second-rate artists: "We can't all play the solo—some of us have to sing in the choir, and there is a great pleasure and a dignity in doing something you love to the best of your ability." I also had to admit that there was a relief, a lifting of a weight like putting down a rucksack; making second-rate anything is far harder and more frustrating than doing it brilliantly, and far less rewarding. It is a series of messily fought retreats spiked with tiny Pyrrhic victories. The realization that throwing in the oily rag meant I no longer had to travel everywhere with a sketchbook fiddling with moody watercolors was like a knocked-out boxer realizing from the canvas that he wasn't going to have to train anymore.

I didn't give up art in a flounce. For the next five or six years, I worked on its periphery, relied on artifice and craft. I painted portraits and murals, did illustration. I thought of being a cartoonist and took a small portfolio of ribaldry to Geoffrey Dickinson, the cartoon editor of *Punch*. He flicked through them, grunted joylessly. "Yes . . . that's been done better. That's not too bad. Nice take on that. Too many words in this one . . ." I was prickly about the intimation that I'd copied jokes, and said so. He regarded me with watery, humorless eyes: "Adrian, *Punch* has been publishing umpteen cartoons every week since 1800 and frozen to death . . . umpteen more are drawn all over the world every day . . . the chance of you coming up with an original one is virtually nil. How long did these take you?" A couple of weeks, I said. "You need to do this amount every day. You need to sell half a dozen a week to make even the most meager living. We pay fifteen pounds a time for full world rights." I thanked him for his advice and dumped the cartoons in the first bin I came to. I felt like the man alone on the desert island who discovers that the water is only ankle deep—and walks off the page.

In my last year at the Slade, I went with my dad to a party at All Souls College in Oxford. It was held on the lawn surrounded by a cloister. I kissed a flushed girl and out of a blue sky a thunderstorm plummeted. The party murmured in that familiar bovine tone of the English surprised by the elements. We moved to the covered walk. In the middle of the lawn, a couple of pulsatingly pulchritudinous undergraduates, both dressed in white cotton, stood in conversation, almost touching, engrossed with each other, in their moment unaware of or unconcerned with the carpet-rod, crashing and flashing rain that rendered them translucent, cloth clinging to bosom and buttock and biceps as on a Greek votive statue. The rest of us watched, the murmur of conversation dipped and died, there was a collective understanding, a quiet satisfaction that the little tableau of panache and élan was also an Oxford moment. After a long minute, the couple looked up as if suddenly back in the temporal world, laughed and slowly sauntered to shelter, she with a hand of ownership resting lightly on his shoulder. The party drifted up the road for tea at Magdalen. As I walked into the street, a bald man with thick-rimmed spectacles asked if I'd like to share his umbrella. "Are you an undergraduate here?" I told him I was at the Slade. Are you a teacher here? I inquired in return. "No. I'm the librarian at Hull." Oh God, I blurted, you're Philip Larkin. He looked uncomfortable, either with the fact or with its disclosure. We got to the college and he asked if I'd seen the chapel. No, I said. He opened a door and there it was, the chapel silently reciting the last line from his "Arundel Tomb." "Our almost-instinct, almost true: / What will survive of us is love." Larkin looked in with the cursory glance of a janitor. "Well, here it is," he said, turned, shook his umbrella and walked smartly away.

I would occasionally go to Oxford parties. As art students, we sneered at the blinky and fey erotically inept and culturally backward undergraduates with intellectual self-confidence and social learning difficulties. Early one morning I left a hall of braying conceit and spavined dancing, drunk, with a girl, and stumbled over the collapsed awkward heap of bicycles that collected against every piss-colored wall. I picked one up and flung it over the wall into a meadow. It was chained to the next bike and that was attached to the next and the next—an unending metal scrum of bikes. I pulled and pushed them over the wall—they seemed such a perfect simile for undergraduates, chained together for safety and assurance, the implication the possibility of inquisitive forward movement, the reality a collective comforting stasis. The girl laughed, which I suppose had been the point.

Years later I was there again to see my daughter Flora get her degree, be transmogrified from graduand to graduate, as some professor kept saying with the smugness of a guard in a stately home. And I remembered the party and the thunderstorm and my dead dad and Larkin and the flushed girl I kissed, the one who laughed, and I thought how different the university seemed, for me at least. It had passed through the invisible door between Gothic and Renaissance. Flora beamed in her ridiculous hat as we posed for photographs, the center of this landscape, a divine atheist with her degree in theology. When I left the Slade, I didn't bother to rent a mortarboard, or queue up to get my diploma . . . I don't think any of us did.

Those who should know and ought to tell rarely tell you

anything useful. At colleges and universities, they tell you used things, things that had a use, were used, until they were used up and are now useless. Passed on like bus tickets for journeys that are already over. Being a student is to be shown things that don't work anymore, that aren't funny or tragic or frightening or relevant anymore. Nobody tells you that the real value of education is taking out the rubbish—a misconception collection. That the most important lessons to learn are what to discard, what you don't need, what doesn't fit. The baggage of secondhand cancerous clothes made for others. What I learned after five years in art school was that I wasn't an artist. Not that I didn't want to be one—I'd never wanted to be anything else—but that I just wasn't. It was the most useful information. I still occasionally see or hear people I was at college with, and all these years later they haven't understood the instruction or read the small print on the label, that they weren't meant to be artists . . . and that the will and the love and the effort and the wishing don't make you one. Knowing what you are not is of far more lasting value than wondering what you are. What you are is what's left when you've cleared everything else away.

Max Liebermann said that the art of drawing was the art of omission. It is a *pensée* that I use more often than any other borrowed quote. It is a powerful truth of life. What you leave out gives the power and the beauty to what is left in; writing is the art of editing, each of these words is the result of a decision not to utilize, call on, pick, substitute, designate, suffer, frog-march, choose other words. I once went down a gold mine two kilometers under the Transvaal where the stone was too hot to touch. A filigree of hundreds of tunnels made over generations had been buried into the Stygian dark blackness, thousands of tons of rock blasted, hewn, shoveled, shifted, crushed, washed and scalded in acid by thousands of miners who worked round the clock all their lives, and it struck me their job wasn't actually mining for gold, it was removing everything that wasn't gold. When they had finished, what was left at the end of the month was enough gold for one man to put in his pocket.

Max Liebermann was a German Impressionist painter, a member of the Berlin Secession, president of the Prussian Academy of Art. They made him a Freeman of the city of Berlin and he was a Jew. In 1933, he watched the Nazis parade through the Brandenburg Gate and said, "I can't eat as much as I would like to puke," another memorable quote. He died in his sleep two years later, stripped of all his posts, his honors, his position. Forced to sell his house, an *Untermensch*. His widow was sent a letter telling her to prepare to travel to Theresienstadt concentration camp. As the Gestapo arrived, she committed suicide beneath the portrait her husband had painted of her in happier times. The art of drawing and the art of life is the art of omission. What we leave out. Who we leave out.

7

My earliest memory: a lawn. Outside our little flat in Stanmore. I'm being told to run . . . run, Adrian, run. A voice behind me. Running must be a novelty, a new thing. Run Adrian run. A girl's voice. I start to run. It's awkward. I'm wearing dungarees, and as I set off across the grass, a hand catches the straps and pulls me back. The girl laughs. Run Adrian run. And I set off again, and I'm caught. Run Adrian run. I don't know when this memory arrived—no one else can corroborate it. It has no provenance. Who is the girl? And the age I must be would seem too young for memories. Also, as I remember it, I can see myself. I stand apart, my striped trousers, the Start-rite shoes, but I can't see my face, nor the girl. Dispassionately, forensically, it doesn't stand up as a reputable memory. It's not a runner. I don't believe I remember it at all. I don't trust the remembrance, but it has always been my earliest memory, the foundation of the great edifice of monolithic experience. But it's a figment, a fabrication . . . and what's more interesting, more concerning, is, if I was going to make up a first memory, a founding myth, why come up with this one? Of all the earliest memories I could make up, why one that was so obviously replete with Freudian imagery, such a simplistic squib of future anxiety and neurosis? The retrospective clue placed like a blunt implement, the murder weapon at the start of a thriller. It's not as if it vies for its primary status with other memories from my early childhood. I don't have any. That's it. This one figure—me on the lawn failing to run, the laughter of a teasing woman. What I know of my childhood is built from photographs, like a smartly edited documentary. I montage the black-and-white images of my early life into a sort of story, not with a plot or a sense of belonging or pleasure. Here's me and my red pedal car; tied to the back is an orange-box cart with my brother sitting in it. I'm supposed to pull him. My father made the cart with old scooter wheels. It's the only mechanical, practical thing my father ever made. It doesn't work. My brother is too heavy, so we just pose for the picture, looking cold and furious. I don't think it's a photo of us, I think it's a picture of my father's orange box with wheels. It's always cold in my montage memory. I'm constantly wrapped in boiled wool, awkward arms, stiff hands pushed into mittens on string. Life is wet and muddy and smells of leaf mold; our home is tiny, a tiny slice of an ugly red-brick Georgian house, a living room we call the big room—this is the age before irony—a kitchen, a bathroom. Upstairs, two bedrooms and a box room with a skylight that is not much more than a cupboard, which is mine. What do I remember? The big room was green and cream. There was a bay window, G Plan furniture, a sideboard with sticky bottles, napkin rings, my father's medals, a television and a Queen Anne cabinet with doors, a radiogram. I remember my first record—Britten's *The Young Person's Guide to the Orchestra* on one side, and Holst's *Planets* on the other. Then *Peter and the Wolf*, declaimed by Peter Ustinov, Sibelius's *Karelia Suite* . . . This is where I had my first drink. I can still taste Crabbie's Ginger Wine. The merest sticky gloss on my milk teeth from the tiny thistle-shaped liqueur glass my grandmother used, clinking on her aquamarine ring and her carmine nails. She liked ginger wine and she liked crème de menthe. "Green lights," she called them, and they reminded her of the club in India where her brother had gone to be a tea planter and she'd followed with the fishing fleet to perhaps find a husband. But they were all too uncouth, bereft of esprit or poetry. I liked the ginger wine, and at Christmas would be given a little glass of my own. I was also encouraged to drink watered wine, which I didn't like, in what my aspiring family believed to be the French way. I don't have memories of childhood good or ill, just the oppressive presence of a garden, which was the reason we'd moved to this tiny dark house. The great verdure was spooky and unloved. A garden made for dead people who'd planted huge cedars that creaked and keened in the wind and who'd built glass verandas that claimed a tithe of broken-necked thrushes and finches. There was the lake where I caught newts for fascination and revulsion, the great crested males that had spotted diseased stomachs and labial frilly backs and were morbidly cold with sticky feet. And the dragonfly nymphs, ferocious as Norse trolls, that lived in darkness to gut sticklebacks and water beetles. In the evening in the calm, silver water, voles would swim, and occasionally the diamond serpentine head of a grass snake. There was an island where a family of ornamental white geese lived. The gander was the first of God's creatures. It was a bully. A malevolent hissing and strutting pimp who was bigger than me and sought me out. It would wait in ambush behind laurels to honk and flap after me on the gravel paths. I was terrified of the gander. One Christmas, the pond froze and a fox tiptoed onto the island and bit the heads off the geese. We found their decorative corpses on the silent ice. It was ghoulishly macabre, like an atheist Christmas card, and it made me very happy—like the boy in Saki's story "Sredni Vashtar," I sat in front of the glowing hearth eating buttered toast, hymning the gander's demise.

As I write about the garden that loomed over my childhood, which was given to me in place of the semirural childhoods my parents had lived, I realize that this is why Pisanello's *Saint Eustace* meant so much to me. His was the perfect vision of my dystopian acre. I was not yet the center of the landscape, nor yet a visitor in a realm of Elysian glory. I felt lonely and lost. The least adept animal in a system that cared neither for nor about me.

A recovered image of my mother in the garden. Physical, gamine, a thick shock of short black hair with a heavy fringe. Freckles, dark complexion. A witty, interested, boyish face, but provocative, mocking, with an exhibitionist smile that is not altogether humorous. She smiles a lot, my mum, when she's angry or disappointed. She smiles when she disagrees. Her smile can wither or zap like Dan Dare's ray gun. She's dressed in a stripy Breton T-shirt with a crew neck and three-quarter sleeves and slacks with a zip up the side (when did slacks become extinct?), tight on her calves, and flat shoes. The memory is tinted with the watery green glow of old Kodachrome movies. She's playing Jokari. A garden game that was so utterly '60s. A rubber ball on an elastic band secured to the ground. You hit the ball away with a paddle. It bounced and returned and you'd hit it again—or more likely miss it. The game was new. So much of everything I remember was new. A new way of looking at things. Doing things. Being things. The better you were at hitting the ball away, the harder it returned. Right there was a game nullifying newness—the worse you played, the better you played. Jokari was an unsport. Unfun. But it had the postwar enter-all-areas attribute of not being prewar. Newness was everything. I was new. I was the postwar generation. A promise. And everything was new to me. I always understood that my parents were the tomorrow people. Their world needed to be remade, reinvented, retooled, rethought, and nothing was to be repeated. We didn't have a cine camera. I don't know why this memory is seawater-graded like a home movie. My father is lying on the lawn, wearing a pair of blue shorts and espadrilles and an Aertex shirt. He's smoking a pipe and reading. All his life he was never farther than five steps from a book, and he always had a handkerchief. A handkerchief and a book. Body and soul. The hanky, produced with a utilitarian flourish like a carousel mechanic's rag, for the blood, snot and tears of childhood. It was warm, soft, and smelled of sweet tobacco, and I remember his thumb as he handed it to me. He had square, striated, flat-chisel thumbs. The inheritance of some lost rural craft.

This is the part where I have to talk about my family. My mother, over there in the sun, confident, tanned, new; the pock-pock of the little ball that returns to her like a tiny, eager dog to be spanked again. My father letting out puffs of aromatic smoke, a skinny pale dragon. Whatever the captain of that other boat, the one I didn't stop, was going to tell me, it will have come from here. Buried somewhere in this garden. Under the tartan picnic blanket, the Festival of Britain plastic plates, the Nordic-style cutlery, the copies of *Time & Tide* and *Encounter*, and a paperback John Braine or Alan Sillitoe, to a song by Dion or Chubby Checker. I've added a sound track to the home movie—there wasn't outside music, but this is my biopic. My mother is doing the Twist—hands floppy, held away from her thighs like plucked wings, pirouetting on one arched foot as if putting out a cigarette. My mother called me a couple of weeks ago and said, "This memoir, this thing you're writing, it's best if you leave me out. I've been thinking . . . better not say anything." Wouldn't it look strange, you know, an autobiography without a parent? Readers might fill in the mother-shaped hole with conclusions? "No. I don't want to be mentioned. You can be unkind. You think it's funny." I'm tempted to do as she asks—leave her there on the lawn in the fading sea-green light forever, but I shan't. This is not my parents' story anymore; they are no longer new. It's mine. My uncertain, squeamish, rifling-through . . . a personal genealogy of what begat what.

Whenever I am asked, I always say I had a happy childhood.

That I was loved, I was fed and shod, I was valued and listened to. There were boundaries and there were horizons, there were certainties and possibilities, there were holidays and train sets and kites that never flew and lead soldiers and colored pencils. And there was the garden. I realize that when I look back at that childhood, I can't see anything that wasn't perfectly happy in the generally agreed-on National Health scale of childhood contentment that ranges between Dickensian misery and Blytonian ecstasy. Mine was arranged in the middle. Comfortably in the middle. There were no great tragedies, we had indoor plumbing, but it was only recently that somebody asked that annoyingly knowing, soft-voice, tissue-box question, "What did your childhood feel like?" And before I could arrange my face into a sneer, I was back in the garden, shrouded with the cold, lonely sadness, mourning a loss that hadn't happened yet. Sadness comes in a swatch of brown shades. Mine wasn't overwhelming or self-hugging, it wasn't unbearable, a curse or a blight or a cross. Looking back, it's difficult to determine exactly what it was . . . like trying to remember a taste. And I don't know how much I retrospectively contaminated it, like adding a sound track or the lighting, for the sake of anecdote or alliteration. Although my childhood was perfectly happy, it didn't feel happy. It felt lonely and lost. Still, in old age, my two fears are being alone and being lost. They reduce me to a child again. My mother used to tease me with a poem that she'd recite in a little boy's voice. She does a cartoon festival of ear-stabbing voices. The little boy is one of the most shudder-gouging. I couldn't hear it. It would make me cry. I'd shout or leave the room. She thought it was funny. It was funny. I haven't considered the poem for years, but I've just gone and found it.

I'm sittin' on the doorstep,
An' I'm eating bread an' jam,
An' I isn't cryin' really,
Though I 'specks you think I am.

I'm feeling rather lonely,
And I don't know what to do,
'Cos there's no one here to play with,
An' I've broke my hoop in two.

I can hear the child'en playing,
But they sez they don't want me.
'Cos my legs are rather little,
An' I run so slow, you see.

So I'm sittin' on the doorstep,
An' I'm eating bread an' jam,
An' I isn't cryin' really,
Though it feels as if I am.

"The Littlest One" was published in the eponymous book in 1914 by Marion St. John Webb, daughter of Arthur St. John Adcock. St. John Adcock must be a contender for the worst double-barreled name ever. Webb wrote masses of simpering children's books, *The Littlest One* being the most successful. Her bibliography shows that she surfed the high-water mark of Edwardian bathos. Her dad was a poet and an editor of *The*

Bookman, who published *Famous Houses and Literary Shrines of London,* which is interesting in a leathery, cigar-club-bore sort of way, full of ponderously recounted literary anecdotes (the worst kind, even more tedious than hunting anecdotes). It's neatly illustrated by yet another St. Adcock—possibly a brother. I can hear my father in all this. Sometimes as I write, his voice is so clearly in the room, along with the faint whiff of pipe tobacco. What he and I did here was to escape the emotion of that hideous syrupy bilge doggerel with its simpering child's voice. Not because it still pricks me with tears, but because I'm consumed with the shame that it ever did. Daddy has just noticed that Marion St. John Webb died in 1930—a month before her father.

The sadness was a default setting, it was how I expected to be. This was the abiding climate of my internal childhood, and I hoped I would grow out of it. Growing up for me didn't mean growing into someone, it meant growing out of someone. "It wasn't normal, your family—you do know they were different?" my oldest friend, Christopher, said last week. He's waited sixty years to pass that on. We have lunch every two or three years and consequently have remained close. He's known me all my life. Our families were close—we had holidays together. His father was an English professor; we would stay with them in their big, untidy Cambridge house, crammed with cereal bowls and poetry books, sticky with eczema cream and the pervasive comforting smell of insecticide shampoo. Our parents would sit around and talk and talk and talk and talk over one another, in a cappella descants, curating an intellectual, cultural, ivory-tower New Jerusalem, planning and gesticulating, sipping wine, smoking, laying their head in each other's laps, stroking backs, laughing and being new. Our small house and the garden were always full of people who were making New England—concrete poets, journalists, actors, film directors . . . dozens and dozens of actors. I came home from school one day and found the Anglican bishop Trevor Huddleston sitting in the big room; another time, the art critic John Berger lying on the lawn. It was a fiercely intellectual, argumentative, didactic newness. You could get shoved into insignificance by the sharp-elbowed dialectics. They would sit around on Heal's chairs with bottles of Bass and Beaujolais, eating pâté. I remember the '60s as one long gluey genital-whiff terrine—pâté was the new potted meat—the air thick with Gitanes and Dad's pipe humming with pertinence and perspicacity. I grew a stammer, like a fairy-tale curse. A verbal hurdle, a clicking turnstile behind my crooked teeth. I would gape like a landed stickleback and ttttt-tut like a football rattle. A stutter is easily mockable and guiltlessly ignorable. Talk, particularly in our house, was a competitive sport. You had to defend your airspace with volume and fluency, commitment, humor, originality and footnotes. There was no quarter given for children. The worst thing about the stammer is the dark mire of frustration and anguish that fluently and logorrheically collects behind the dam of the tongue, creating a great unsaid reservoir and terrible bitter *esprit d'escalier*. I would mutter vainglorious ripostes to myself on the front step. I invented an imaginary friend to tell them to—Big Mister. He in turn had his own imaginary friend—

Little Mister, whom he could chat to when he was fed up with listening to me dig graves for *m*'s and *r*'s and *g*'s. But the most infuriating thing about a stammer is that people finish your sentences for you. Usually incorrectly and ungrammatically, with the irritated charity of helping to get a pram onto a bus. There is an unstuttered assumption that stammering is the audible symptom of a simple mind, the reversing beep of cretinism. It is, alternately, funny and irritating. Nobody has ever taken someone else's stammer seriously as a disability—and that is another reason why it is such a torment. If you try to explain a stammer, someone else will butt in to finish your self-pity for you. I went to a health center recently that by chance housed the National Health's stammering unit. A public relations officer told me it was named after its patron, Michael Palin, because Palin had played a comic character with an imitation stutter in *A Fish Called Wanda*. I stood there open-mouthed, once again rendered speechless. It's like naming the Commission for Racial Equality after Al Jolson, a white guy who blacked up to entertain folk, or naming a mute's charity after Sooty . . . or, indeed, the Commission for Racial Equality after Sooty. I was sent in search of a therapist to ease my blockage, which was generally agreed to be wholly mechanical and possibly willful. Miss Love was a breathy and suggestive willful woman with barely sweatered intercontinental breasts, intense dark eyes and a lot of black hair arranged into a complicated bouffant. It took ages and two buses to get to her treatment room. Mum used to take me. And along the way we'd scan the pavement for hair grips. I can't remember why we started collecting them, but you'd be astonished how many bobby pins were lost in the street in the '60s.

BOBBY—OR BOBBED—PINS WERE INVENTED at the end of the nineteenth century for a new bobbed hairstyle, crimped by Robert "Bobby" Pinot. If he'd called his 'do a "Pinot," they could have been "pin pins." In England, they were known as Kirby grips, after the Birmingham firm of Kirby Beard & Co. Ltd. Again a mere inverting whim and they could have been "beard grips." Miss Love terrified me with her provocative, softly spoken *Carry On* sensuality. Our therapy sessions consisted of me lying on an examination table while she told me to relax in a Fenella Fielding voice, and would then touch my woolly foot and say "foot" with a great heaving zephyr of emotion. I was supposed to repeat "foot," which I usually managed, and then she'd lay her warm hand on my shin "shin," "sh-sh-sh-shin," "knee," "kn-kn-kn-knee," "thigh," "th-th-th-th-thigh," and the hand would glide to my tummy. "Tummy," "t-t-t-tummy." I was not a credit to Miss Love's siren repetition therapy.

My parents never treated me like a child. I was always paid the double-edged compliment of an assumption of equality, that intellectually, at least, there would be no shallow end in my childhood. By the time I got to junior school, I knew all the Greek and Nordic myths because my father had told them to me as bedtime stories. My parents wanted to be different from their parents, to be free of the dogma and the worries, the little snobberies and etiquette embarrassments. And they would do this by being true to themselves to an existential degree that would have made Sartre tip his *chapeau* in admiration. They constructed a mold for a modern way of being together. They fought, and both had lovers. I can't remember a time in my life when I didn't know the facts of life and the facts of my parents' love life. I knew many of my father's girlfriends, and my mother's long-term boyfriend is still a man I'm very fond of. Terry was an important person in my life. He was a marvelous illustrator who taught me how to draw. And whilst it wasn't so much an open marriage as a drafty one, neither was it always amicable or even or terribly sophisticated. It was unquestionably selfish and egotistical, but it was also immense fun and exciting. It just wasn't ideal for kids. I have friends who complain, ruefully, that their parents never told them they loved them. Everybody in our house got told they were loved, constantly. If you came to read the meter, someone would have loved what you were doing. I was told I was loved on an hourly basis. It was the signal for what came next, which could be vicious. Declarations of love were the permission to impart colder, steelier home truths. There was an emotional openness, a stream of consciousness bordering on incontinent that was brave and liberated and definitely new, but it was the Wild West of child care. All love was tough.

It's been said that you understand your parents only when you become one. I must say, four children later, I haven't been offered any revelations about my childhood. But I am more aware of the obvious fact that all parents are themselves children and of what my mother and father came from and went through to become my parents. Which is far more telling than where we all ended up. They were born at either end of the Depression, my mother in Edinburgh, my father in Kent—though his parents were immigrants from Batley in the West Riding of Yorkshire. My paternal grandfather's father was a semiliterate, semiskilled agricultural and mill laborer. His son my grandfather George Arnold Gill did well at school. His teacher said he had a chance of going to university. George Arnold dreamed of being a doctor. Medicine and college were unheard-of leaps in class and presumption that would have meant years of unearning study. The local bank manager knocked on the door and said he'd heard that George Arnold was a bright boy, and that if he came to the bank, he could have an indoor, collar-and-tie job as a junior clerk and bring in a wage right away. They wouldn't have to bother with the expense and the worry and the fear of university, where he'd be mocked by his betters. So his father delivered George Arnold to the bank. He was a clever and diligent boy. In 1914 he joined the British Expeditionary Force, and he fought through the war, going into the newly formed tank regiment. I think he was at the Battle of Cambrai. There was a story passed down in the family that he had been recommended for a decoration—being the most forward British officer in the battle—but was not given it for failing to shoot his own sergeant, who had run back to the line when their tank was hit by shell fire. The story didn't come from him; he rarely talked about the war. I remember him as a kindly, gentle, round-faced man with a white mustache who would carve the beef on Sundays and always dip a triangle of bread into the blood, sprinkle it with salt and solemnly pass it down the table to me. This now seems more allegorically profound than it did at the time. The blood sacrament from the roast beef of old England, the salt and the bread of welcome and belonging, the blood bond of sacrifice and duty, the obligation of transubstantiation, redemption, rebirth and a new generation. Sunday lunch with three generations of family was my grandfather's quiet victory and memorial. I can still taste it, the warm bread, metallic with blood and salt, life and tears, like a slap in the mouth, a kiss on the lips. What I remember about him was the gentle, unassuming dignity. The carving of the meat, the ritual of the box with the knife and fork, the sharpening of the blade, steel on steel, the reverence for the flesh, the compliments to the gravy, and being handed down the sop. A gift, a bond and acknowledgment from my grandfather to me. It was the first time I'd tasted the great-altar truth of the table that food is far more than what is on your plate.

After lunch he would sit in his armchair and sleep. When he woke, he would peel an orange with a small silver pocketknife and give me segments, and I'd march up and down with his walking stick. The war was a constantly stoically borne ghostly tinnitus. He'd been wounded. His inseparable best friend had been killed beside him—they had considered shooting their thumbs off to escape the trenches. He remained a member of the British Legion, kept in touch with old comrades, but they were a secret society who guarded great unfathomable sorrow and pride. Every old man I knew had been in the Great War, and they all kept the *omertà* of silence. But I would notice that they did small things—furling an umbrella, knotting a tie, closing a gate—with the slow, reverential care of a guilty pleasure. My grandfather brushed his thin hair with a pair of silver-backed brushes and the attention of an undertaker preparing a client. A daily ritual with the mirror that I suppose said, "I live, others didn't." He was an exceptionally tender man. I only once saw him nearly give in to anger. The local hunt chased a fox through his garden, the hounds and horses breaking his remembrance of pruned roses and churning up his even more carefully tended lawn. His anger wasn't at the destruction, but at the blatant bullying, the unfairness of the pursuit. And I suspect something in him identified with the fear and the desperate no-man's-land dash of the fox.

While he was away in the trenches, the bank employed local girls to be clerks; the one who took my grandfather's place sent him parcels of cigarettes, chocolates and socks. Mary was a local farmer's daughter. The family had a milk round, with churns on a horse-drawn cart. They had come down in the world. Her grandparents and uncles had owned mills that made shoddy, recycled wool. Batley had hundreds of shoddy mills and shoddy magnates. One of my great-great-uncles managed to drink away the business before he was thirty and then signed the pledge. Batley was a fervently Methodist town with a large Zion temple and very few pubs.

MARY WAS ENGAGED to a young man who'd been sent to the Dardanelles. He contracted a fever and was dispatched back to

England on a hospital ship, which took the long way round through the Suez Canal and down the coast of Africa, but he didn't make it. Died at the Cape. The news was telegraphed to her, but the letters he'd written home and posted on the way took much longer to find her. They were full of the jolly, larky sentiment that is the inexplicable leitmotif of the time. His mother was reduced to the asylum. Mary was buttoned-down and stoical, hardly alone in her bereavement. She continued at the bank, and in 1919, a man came to her teller's window, smiled and said thank you for the socks. They were married shortly afterward. George Arnold prospered at the bank, becoming its youngest manager and moving south to Canterbury. My grandmother was very Yorkshire. The general perception of Yorkshire people is loud and sardonic and confident. Actually, that's just folk from Leeds. Mary was shy but steely, tough and wary. She had had scarlet fever as a child that nearly did for her. It left her alive, but very deaf. She didn't like showing off or overt displays of anything. She wasn't good in a room or with crowds, she was very private, but she loved her family and doted on my father, who was to be her only child. A prospective sister was miscarried late. My father, George Michael, was a sickly boy. He contracted tuberculosis and spent years of his childhood in a spinal chair being pushed around by a young tutor. He was shortsighted, had few friends—just a fox terrier called Patch who was run over by a fire engine. The '30s ground on, the war arrived, Canterbury was hit in a Baedeker raid: the bombing of culturally significant cities highlighted in a German tourist guide—today they'd be called TripAdvisor drones.

George Arnold and George Michael walked through their flaming city to see that the cathedral still stood, and my dad joined the Royal Air Force. He wrote a book about it that was published just as he died. The war preoccupied him at the end of his life. It was, as it must have been for anyone who lived through it, the defining experience, the barometer against which all cultural and political life was measured. He had a tough time in the RAF, he was still weak and too shortsighted for air crew, and he was bookish and left-wing and cerebral and a solitary mummy's boy. The other recruits mocked and hazed him, but he was utterly committed and believed in the struggle for European civilization. Photographs of him show a serious, handsome young man, self-contained. He sat the officers' exam, in which he was asked what he would do having shot down a plane if the pilot ejected safely and was floating back to enemy territory. Aircraftman 2nd Class Gill wrote that he would let him land. The immediate threat had passed, the individual battle had been won, and to machine-gun an un-threatening helpless enemy was simply morally wrong. The war was bearable only if we were better, superior to the enemy. If we weren't fighting for the rightness of our culture, then it was all merely about power and gold. It was the wrong answer. The pilot was worth more than the plane. To let him go to fight again was to possibly pay for your scruples with someone else's life later on. Winning was too important to be risked by the niceties of chivalry. My father was sent back to the grueling obstacle course to reconsider.

He became an officer, and the only person who fired a shot

at him personally in anger was an Irish Republican whilst he was on guard duty at Stormont in Belfast. He joined a daylight bomber squadron of Mitchells as an intelligence officer and went on raids in support of D-day. At the end of the war he took part in the occupation of Germany, and this, as much as anything, forged the person he was to become. He talked a lot about the destruction of Cologne, of the millions of liberated homeless, lost, and bereft people setting off to walk back to somewhere that might or might not be home, to families and friends who might or might not still live. Millions of starved, weak, desperate, slave laborers, camp survivors, the displaced, misplaced, unplaced and shocked, walking hundreds of miles through a catastrophically damaged continent. He was never in any doubt of how close we'd come to destroying our civilization. Years later, he made the TV series *Civilisation* with Kenneth Clark. The first episode, called *The Skin of Our Teeth*, looked at the Dark Ages and how classical civilization had nearly perished. Clark had been the young director of the National Gallery—during the war an empty gallery, the pictures hidden in mines in Wales. Both of them understood how dark the '30s and '40s had been and how civilization had been wrested from barbarism by the skin of our teeth again.

Like George Arnold, George Michael had wanted to be a doctor, but he gave up a place reading medicine at Guy's Hospital school and took a short postwar degree at Edinburgh reading philosophy and psychology—two subjects he thought a new world would be in greater need of—and there he met a young actress who was an ingenue star of Scottish theater.

My mother's mother, May Bailey, came from a working-class family of Scots skilled laborers. She had a hard childhood, having to sell papers door-to-door. Her father was a drunk who could be violent, her mother a characteristically unforgiving woman. May was beautiful—poised and dramatic and romantic and ambitious. She was Miss West of Scotland in an early beauty and talent contest, and a ladies' golf champion who sang amateur opera. She would have liked to be professionally dramatic, but somehow never managed to make it more than a wish. She worked as a secretary for Sir William Mac-Taggart at the National Gallery of Scotland and tried to find or keep a man who would be a suitable husband. At the close of the First War, there was a shortage, and I expect my grandmother had exacting standards. In the end, she went for a French dentist. I never knew my grandfather. He wasn't French, he was Mauritian and half Indian. I look at photographs of him and wonder how anyone could have imagined him anything other than Asian or African. But in Edinburgh before the war, he passed for white and French. He wasn't a qualified dentist, either. He fought in the war and said that he'd turned down a commission because he wished to remain with the men, though he did have himself photographed in an officer's greatcoat.

I think my grandparents' marriage was not altogether what it appeared to be, or what either of them wanted or expected. He came to Scotland to study engineering, but the family firm of Coopers back in Port Louis failed, swallowing his inheritance. There was no money to finish his degree, so he became not exactly a dentist but a tooth-puller down by the docks in Leith. He had pretensions to being a country gent, kept a Labrador, dressed in tweed, went shooting and fishing, had wanted my mother to be a boy. Yvonne Jeannette was an only child who took her mother's thwarted ambitions and made them professional. She left school at fifteen and joined a theater company, becoming a successful juvenile lead, doing panto and rep, comedy and tragedy and radio broadcasts. She was beautiful and vivacious. And her father died. Dropped dead in the street. It was suggested that the worry about the imminent National Health Service gave him a heart attack, which is a dark irony.

By the time I knew her, my maternal grandmother was a dear and exotically eccentric woman of a sort that's not uncommon in the new town of Edinburgh. She bore an air of disappointment and lily of the valley. She had mauve hair, cerise hats, a leopard-print lamb's-wool coat, puce lipstick and a deathly white face with rouged cheeks and large kohl-smudged eyes, pearl earrings, aquamarine rings, support stockings and elasticated bloomers. Gran was a martyr to her circulation. She had tired blood. She had also been martyred by circumstances and fate, bravely enduring ill luck, usually by singing snatches of show tunes in a trilling Edwardian voice and filling in betting slips. She lived with my great-aunt Netta, her constant, dowdier companion, whose role in life was to make tea and offer commiserations and who died a virgin, having been let down by a merchant seaman at some point in the distant past. I adored them both. I used to take Netta on pub crawls when I was a student. She was happy to sit in a corner with a sherry and be treated like an exotic visitor from another age. "Oh," she'd sigh, "you're all such bright and vivacious young things. Adrian, have fun while you can, don't be like me and save everything for a sunnier day. Spend it all now." And I did.

My parents must have been a glamorous couple in Edinburgh. They married. I was born in the Royal Infirmary, where Burke and Hare sold their corpses in the nineteenth century, and baptized in the Church of Scotland for the sake of the grandparents—my mother and father were atheists. My dad worked as a journalist and a subeditor on *The Scotsman*. He got a job as an arts reporter on BBC radio and we moved to London, where my mother lived with me in a room with a shared kitchen and bathroom in Chelsea whilst my father did a producer's course to make television. They bought the little flat with the big garden in Stanmore and my paternal grandparents helped pay for the furniture, suggesting the Georgian-style reproductions that they lived with, but my mother insisted on G Plan. It was modern, it was new. And I began growing up. My father moved to television and became an immensely successful and innovative documentary maker. My mother gave up acting until I was eleven and then returned to the stage, also making television and films—*Z Cars* and *Crossroads*, *Fawlty Towers*, Dr. Finlay and Alan Bennett, *Empire of the Sun*, *Chariots of Fire*—but working mostly in London's energetic fringe theater of the '70s. And then she became a venerable speech coach, particularly championing women's public voices, and was made a Fellow of the Saïd Business School and Imperial College.

When I think of my parents as children—rather than the parents of my brother and me—I have pockets full of admiration for the distance they traveled. How much of their lives was self-invented. How much of it was not into the unknown but into the barely known . . . or the just imagined and the deeply mistrusted. They wanted to get as far as they could from the life that they had been brought up in and that their parents represented. Not just those specific lives, but the collective life from before the war, with its fears and net-curtain certainties, its sentimental snobberies and social insecurity. All that was left behind. They and the generation of young, socialist, atheist, intellectually modernist, international men and women wanted to forge a better, improved, freer, more humane, less hypocritical template for living. One that was open to individualism and difficult ideas that questioned every orthodoxy and all tradition that offered liberty along with care.

My father was born in 1923, the year Stanley Baldwin first became prime minister. The BBC made its first outside broadcast on the wireless, *The Magic Flute*; Tutankhamen's tomb was opened; a patent for the television tube was filed in America; *The Inimitable Jeeves* was published. My father died in 2005. The BBC broadcast *Jerry Springer: The Opera* on television; fox hunting was banned; Harold Pinter won the Nobel Prize for literature, and Tony Blair was elected prime minister for the third time. That represents an enormous gamut, a social, political, cultural and emotional marathon, and millions of people made and lived through it. But the distance both my parents moved from the certainties of their birth to the possibilities of now was far, far greater than I have had to travel from 1954 to my sixtieth birthday. My cultural and intellectual and social leap is tiny compared with theirs, a mere tinkering with the model they created for me, for us.

The generation that came out of the second war made a far better fist of rebuilding Europe than the one that emerged from the First War. And though their generation is derided and blamed for everything from drugs to moral turpitude, woolly thinking and unpolished shoes, they encouraged and allowed a period that has been as exciting and creative as any comparable time since the fourteenth century. And I have never had to wear khaki. They were, though, a self-service generation. My father and mother were both self-serving, self-justifying, self-interested and, in varying degrees at various times, selfish and solipsistic in that the greatest truth was always in being true to yourself, and the greatest hypocrisy was to compromise yourself. It didn't necessarily make for a warm and tender home, but I am the product, for good and ill, of their experiment. A new life that has had more things to cleave to than to rue. And just as they didn't want to be like their parents, so I don't want to be like mine.

8

I was sent to the local infant school. I remember only a knee-scouring, elbow-serrating, child-hating exercise yard after the fearful wild freedom of my garden. It was confusing; full of knots and scuffs of boys and constant sniveling. The one clear memory is of a little girl, blond with a chapped pink face. It's winter. Frosty and wet. She's wearing thick woolly gray gloves, there's snot streaming from her nose, down onto her puffy, peeling lips, and she bites the gloves' fingers one by one to pull them off; the sticky, itchy wool is smeared with the rime of head goo and drizzle, her teeth tugging the claggy, choking digits, and as if she were telling runes, casting bones or incanting spells, instantly I was struck down with a compulsive aversion to gloves . . . and to wool rubbing against wool. It became almost a phobia. Still I can't wear socks without shoes. I really don't like being in a room with anyone who does . . . the idea of bed socks is horrifying and it meant that I never managed to keep a pair of gloves on. If I wore a glove, I couldn't think of anything but the glove. It was like having a spider on my hand, and I would have to keep my hands permanently in my pockets.

Then, in my late forties, I gave up smoking—this had nothing to do with the gloves—and took up frantic nicotine chewing. I mentioned to my dentist that I was growing breasts on the side of my face. He told me that was no joke and I might break my jaw with a stress fracture and I thought this was silly. By chance, the hypnotist Paul McKenna lived round the corner. I bumped into him on the street and asked, could he stop my nicotine cudding? "Of course," he said, and I spent half an hour being relaxed and deprogrammed and recalibrated and positively reinforced. And as I was there, I wondered if he could cure my allergy to gloves. "What's it like?" he said. It's like claustrophobia for hands, a gagging, digital panic. "What's the first image you associate with gloves?" I told him about the little snot girl and the chewing wool, and he spoke softly and clearly and filled my head with positive haberdashery thoughts and refused to take any payment, saying that it was a gift to me from the universe through him. He wouldn't charge me for it, but I might give something to charity. I left his mews house and never chewed nicotine gum again . . . or smoked. And now I can happily wear gloves—though still not woolen ones. Leather, suede, kid and Pecari are all grand. But there was a price apart from the charitable one, a reckoning, as there always is with magic, when you dabble in the mysteries of the universe and the caprice of unseen powers. Paul fitted me up with a secret and equally irrational passion . . . for buying gloves. I can't pass a pair without reaching for my credit card. I have enough gloves to accouter an opposable-thumbed millipede.

After infant school, it was off to the Church of England

state junior about half a mile down the hill. I walked there miserably. I was not popular at school, and school was not popular with me. I was a weedy, skinny boy who'd never kicked a ball with skill or glorious intent. We didn't play football at home— my father didn't support a team, so neither did I. We would play gentle bouts of French cricket, a sport that never, ever, in the history of compulsory universal education has been played in an English state school playground. My first game on tarmac was Spitfires and Messerschmitts, which is basically tag with extended arms and machine-gun noises; and then regular bouts of British Bulldog and Red Rover, always on the fringe . . . to make up the numbers. If there was picking sides, I would be last or next to last. "We'll take Wilko, you can have Gill and the hop-along with the calipers." The only member of my family who was any good at sports was my mother, who won the mothers' race three years in a row, running barefoot, miles ahead of the other, lumpen wives. All our teachers were men who'd had "good wars"—a couple had limps, one a shell-shocked compulsive blink. I was surprisingly dim at school. I say surprisingly—it didn't come out of the sun for me. I was clever enough to know I knew very little indeed and understood less. I think it was a surprise for my parents, who assumed that I would be at least effortlessly brilliant. Most of the other boys were from the RAF camp that still dotted this bit of Middlesex around what had been Fighter Command at Bentley Priory. Most of them had been to four or five schools and were well traveled to the last reluctant dabs of Empire: Aden, Malaya, Cyprus. The school's academic attainment wasn't high—not that anyone was counting in those days. We were on the cusp of all the great changes in education, the waves of isms and projects and protocols, new ways of being, new horizons. St. John's was a modern, low, timidly brutal, cheap school built to serve the new commuter belt. We were aimed at the 11+ exam, taken in our final year of primary school, without much hope of hitting it, and were taught in a strange hybrid of ancient and modern. Our slanting desks with fold-up lids had inkwells that were filled every week, and we learned to write with dip pens, both cursive and italic script—not just pointless but counterintuitive, to train your hand one way and then force it another. We didn't do Latin, but we did do a lot of religious education. Secondary modern schools were turning into comprehensives and education was becoming child-centered rather than subject-, teacher- or relevance-centered. But it all made little difference to me, I was spectacularly stupid. Remedial at everything. We did old maths, imperial, fractions, and we chanted tables. I memorized the tune; I can still hum it today, but I never got the words. My best subject was the nature table, because I brought in the shiversome newts with their uterine flanged backs. I was moderately bullied. There were kids more noticeably tormentable than me. This being the first decade of the National Health, there were still plenty of Victorian ailments to go round; every class had a child who just survived polio, there were lots of cross-eyed kids with sex-toy-pink round specs or big clip-on hearing aids. Many were noticeably poor. The only diversity was a pair of Jewish boys who weren't allowed into assembly—they sat in the hall so as not to sully the hymns. One of them walked home the same way as me and would pick on me. I was very frightened of him and used to run ahead or hang back, but one day he followed me to the front gate and I can still conjure the panicky sense of outrage at the trespass. We fought in front of my home, in my fearful secret garden. I cried great hopeless, terrified, shamed sobs, sat on his chest, dribbled streamers of spit and tears and punched his face. He went home snarling; I sniveled. It was the only fight I've ever won, and it didn't make me want to try again.

We were given IQ tests—the reductive and absurd measurement of nothing terribly useful. Their original purpose had been to ascertain which hillbilly hick immigrant volunteer to America's scratch army for World War I might make a good NCO, because so many of them were semiliterate or spoke English clumsily. A test was needed that wasn't based on a common academic curriculum but still measured a certain intuition and awareness. It turned out that I was a prodigious whiz at IQ tests. No one actually told me that I was good at them, the results of IQ tests were secret and exchanged on a need-to-know basis. Among those who didn't need to know were the children who'd done them. I still don't know what my IQ was or is. Every other achievement at school would be announced with rare pride at assembly, to applause and ribbons. But IQs were thought to be slightly sinister and private and unfair. Unearned. It was, after all, *despite* the best endeavors of teachers—you didn't acquire your intelligence by hard work, paying attention and doing what you were told. Intelligence was like penis size— undeserved and best kept to yourself. So my parents were summoned and told confidentially that I had an unusually and, it must be said, surprisingly big one. And as the school expected IQ to march in step with achievement, there must be some reason why I didn't shine. So, I wasn't just stupid, I was willful. Was everything all right at home? they asked. Was there some trauma, some wretched secret? A bereavement? Inherited deviance or weakness? Anything that might account for my ability to make connections between inverted geometric shapes and identify synonyms but utterly fail to master the three times table. So I went back to the bus stop for another boring and humiliating journey to see another softly spoken concerned creepy professional, a child psychologist who let me play with toys while he watched over interlaced fingers. They weren't actually genetically correct abuse dolls, but the '60s equivalent— Bauhaus modernist wooden bricks. I made camps and fortresses and was asked why I wanted all the dolls to die in a crossfire, so I just stopped talking to him, turned my back and looked at the pictures in the *Beano* comic books. "Adrian, are you ignoring me for a reason? Adrian, is there something that's upsetting you that you can't say out loud?" After weeks of this, they decided I had a new condition, a brand-new disease, box-fresh from America. Dyslexia.

If I'd been born a couple of years later, I might have been given toxic shock syndrome. Go and type "dickslixia" into Google and you'll be confronted with 11,700,000 entries— that's the population of Belgium talking of little but bad spelling. Word blindness was first discovered, inevitably, by a German. A nineteenth-century optician called Berlin. The German language is dyslexia's Everest. He wondered why some people found it difficult to read, but had perfect eyesight. He thought it was a consequence of brain damage and coined the classical name. It really got going in the twentieth century with universal education, particularly in the English-speaking world. It seems to be a genetic weakness in our tongue—the way Gaucher's disease preys on the Ashkenazi Jews. Apparently there is no dyslexia in China, it doesn't occur in languages that use pictograms and is less prevalent in ones where the spelling and grammar are logical. They say that the Chinese word for dyslexia is the glyph for "word" but reversed. In the '60s, the big problem for dyslexics wasn't that nobody understood what we wrote, but that hardly anyone believed dyslexia existed—certainly very few schoolteachers—it might have been invented by seditionary children to undermine everything teachers stand for. What is the point of teaching that strivers will prosper and slackers will flounder, if the strivers might still drown in the Niagara of words through no fault of their own and despite the best efforts, skill and bullying of the teacher? Dyslexia is a psychobabble heresy to the orthodox belief in education. Like IQ tests, it undermines the doxology that if you do as I say, you will prosper, that education is truly the meritorious road to culture, commerce and being a better person. Dyslexia isn't a mental illness or a condition that affects behavior or temper or mood, you can't look at someone and say, "They seem to be a touch dyslexic"; it is a condition of childhood that manifests itself only in schools. Dyslexics aren't born feeling stupid or failures. Their self-worth and optimism isn't dented until they get to a classroom. Dyslexia is a personal, ingrate slight to everything teachers and teaching stand for. So here I was with a stammer and this new condition, in a family that valued books and words above all else, that had used education to improve its lot for two hard generations—what were they to do with this tongue-tied, word-curdled boy?

Among the sepia washed-out memories, I vividly recall my interview at St. Christopher School, Letchworth, Herts. The headmaster, Mr. King-Harris, took me into his study, just the two of us. He was one of those supremely confident men that English boarding schools made and then kept to make more. A twinkling, avuncular, encouraging man who skillfully mixed sympathetic kindness with a sort of muscular joshing that occasionally drifted into bullying. These Arnold-inspired teachers were all about finding the person inside yourself, as if personal development were an internal dressing-up box. You could try on the character of a better man than you were shaping up to be. They themselves were invariably un-self-aware, having pristinely unexamined lives, having never known a doubt; their confidence was God-given and came with a cast-iron, copper-bottomed, golden guarantee of steely religion. King-Harris was a Quaker. St. Christopher's was a Quaker school that prided itself on finding the inner man or woman in the most unpromising child. It was also one of the few institutions in the country that claimed to be able to cure dyslexia. It was fee-paying and private. King-Harris saw an exploitable market, pioneering the monetizing of middle-class dyslexia anxiety. He spoke kindly to me about this spelling thing and said,

"Let's see how you manage." He handed me a daily paper—
The Guardian, obviously—and asked me to read the top story.
The Commonwealth Prime Ministers' Conference was on at
the time, and the first paragraph seemed to be a list of African
and Asian names. I stuttered and stabbed for a couple of minutes, then handed the paper back. "No, no, don't give up,"
King-Harris said, with his enthusing, teasing voice. And he led
me through the names one at a time, letter by letter, compound-
ing the humiliation and thick hopelessness. Having reduced an
eleven-year-old to the edge of tears, he smiled, folded up the
paper and said, "I think you could do very well here, Adrian.
I'd better have a word with your father. Will you wait outside?" So I sat outside in the stark but well-made hall. Quakers
are very fond of carpentry, a snug dovetail joint encompassed
their temporal and spiritual view.

We couldn't really afford school fees and St. Christopher's
were particularly excessive, but again, there was the absolute
belief in the absolute goodness of education. My parents agreed
to find them. My mother went back to work. Neither of them
ever mentioned the money, ever made me feel responsible or
guilty or indebted, but of course I knew. Not least because
boarding school was never an option for my brother. It was an
odd decision to privately educate one child and send the other
to a local comprehensive, to banish one and keep the other at
home. Both of us felt hurt and bereft by this. Nick, that he was
given less than me; he went from being one of a pair to an only
child. We were close in the way that brothers who squabble
and compete are, but I felt cast out as he got the attention of

our parents, and felt that I was being punished for my imbecility. It seems worse in retrospect than it did at the time. During the war, lots of families were split up, children sent hither and yon. It wasn't so unusual. And this was for a good reason.

My mother took me to school. We didn't own a car; rather than take the train, she got Mr. Button to drive us. Mr. Button was a florid and genial gent who drove a Rover and acted as the local chauffeur for weddings, funerals and snobbery. This was his first trip to a boarding school, so he wore his black suit and chauffeur's cap. My new trunk was unloaded into the spartan dormitory. Two sets of bunk beds that I would share with three other boys in a cold and grubby threadbare hut with a communal bathroom over a concrete playground in the main house. A matron showed me my bed. I went back outside to say good-bye to my mother, but she and Mr. Button had already left. I expect she didn't want to upset me by seeing her cry. I sat on my bed and have never felt quite so utterly, desperately alone. I swore an oath that I would never, ever send a child of mine away.

Even today St. Christopher's is an odd place. In the '60s, it was both utterly bizarre and spot-on the zeitgeist. When people ask if I went to public school, I say yes, but it's really not what you think. It had been started during the First War, in the first Garden City, an idealized town for the future, designed by Ebenezer Howard to be the third place—half urban, half rural, with the best of each, but no pubs. It turned out to be the template for all suburbs. St. Chris, as the school was universally known, had been started by Theosophists, a sort of hedge fund of religions that was cooked up in the mid–nineteenth century around the visions of a Russian aristocrat medium spiritualist and chronic liar who had revelations that all religions were based on a single secret truth which united everything and was overseen by a spirit quango known as the Masters of the Ancient Wisdom. The point of everything was to understand the intelligent evolution of existence and then attain perfection. Unfortunately, the Theosophists couldn't stop splitting up into competing schisms and splinters, so the school was taken over by the ever practical modest and humorless Quakers as part of a broader questioning of the nature and purpose of education. It had some peculiarly extreme principles. Unusually for boarding schools then, but as a great consolation to us, it was coeducational. It was also vegetarian. The only wholly vegetarian boarding school in the country. And organic. Two decades before anyone had ever heard of organic, we grew our own wormy, woody food and kept a herd of uninoculated cows whose bacterially unchallenged, unpasteurized milk was delivered in churns (this was how my father had contracted TB). The vegetarian thing meant that we were encouraged to sell our dung for medical research. We'd shit into plastic bags and get a fiver at the end of term. There was no school uniform. We could wear what we liked—though strangely not jeans. We could grow our hair as long as we wished . . . which was long. One of my friends cropped his hair and dressed in a very authentic SS officer's uniform as his own protest against something or other. He would smartly *Sieg heil* teachers and visitors, pedaling past on his bicycle. The school prided itself on listening to children and that everyone's voice carried equal weight, so we were self-governing. There were layers of councils and committees, including a moot and a judicial committee, all of which were elected by the school, as was every official position from head boy to bell ringer. Voting was by proportional representation on the single transferable vote. Tallying the votes was a nightmare. And there was supposedly no punishment—certainly there was no corporal punishment—the school had proudly pacifist principles. There was, though, Arnold's correctional behavior. If you were caught smoking, you were made to pick up cigarette ends. We could be gated, have meager privileges withdrawn and be rusticated, as I was once for being caught in a girl's dormitory too often; the letter King-Harris sent to my parents was a model of mealy-mouthed liberal manipulation. We called the teachers by their Christian names, except for the headmaster, whom we called Mr. King-Harris. The teachers were a rum bunch of alternative educational zealots and hopeless lost causes who needed the protection of an institution. The all-purpose carpetbag of thwarted and should-have-done-betters that you will find in any private school. They wore sandals with socks all year; some only wore shorts. There was a lot of exclamatory hair, hessian, tweed, flax, hemp, macramé and craft jewelry. One woman remained silent every Wednesday in remembrance of the victims of Hiroshima and Nagasaki. Lessons were compulsory and old-fashioned. The teaching was unremarkable, rote and boring. Despite all the New Age prospectus dressing, it was still an English boarding school with all the concomitant casual bigotry, bullying and solitary misery. We had *exeat* and *Quis?* and *Ego* and all the kiddie prisoners' patois of internment. I was hopelessly homesick. We weren't allowed to phone our parents for three weeks at the beginning of term, and then only from one public pay phone with a permanent queue of rheumy-eyed boys desperate to send their love to the family dog.

My mother kept my letters home. We were made to write every Sunday. Recently she gave them back to me. After half a century, I was completely unprepared for the pang of pitiful unexpressed sadness that radiated from each staccato, uneventful repetitious and awkward page. "Hope you are well, I'm fine. The film was *Dr. Strangelove.* Please give my love to Nick." They all finished with my love to my brother. I'm amazed my mother kept them. I'm amazed she managed to receive them with equanimity—or to give them back to me. Eventually we were all dulled and steeled ourselves to the routine of bells and timetables, found the unlikely pleasure in tiny things: hoarded sweets, a shilling's-worth of head cheese from a local butcher, cold toast and marmalade hidden in a sock drawer. I vividly remember buying my first pomegranate and sitting on my bed in the empty Saturday dormitory eating each iridescent ruby seed with a pin. The school was ugly, run-down, chipped and cracked. And it was cold. The Quaker belief in simplicity and modesty without indulgence or flamboyance, conveniently dovetailed with the public school ethos of character-building, chilly, scratchy, damp bombast. The heating wasn't put on until the first week of November, irrespective of the weather. Baths were had twice a week in secondhand water, the food was foul, cooked by Italians who couldn't understand how the English could treat their children like this. But there were things that were good. Along with my oath not to send my children to boarding school, I also decided that I should be someone else—not to find the person inside me, but simply to pretend to be someone I wasn't, because who I was, was bullied and friendless and plainly failing. And somehow it worked. Like a spy in deep cover, I am still pretending to be the person I made up on a dreary Sunday in September. This character liked being around girls and discovered he was popular. Within a term, his stammer had been swallowed whole. I made friends, started smoking, discovered the contagious excitement of masturbation, then competitive masturbation, along with the great, obsessive-compulsive head-pumping awful pleasure of teenage crushes and the fabulous helter-skelter excitement of pre-almost-fornicatory sex.

THE SCHOOL HAD ANOTHER contrary ideal—noncompetition. We were cooperative, not competitive. Life wasn't about who came first, but how you helped those who were last. No one would eat till the last person was at the table. It drove the games teacher to distraction. I remember a football game where our first XI had finally found a visiting team who were worse at the beautiful game than we were, and when the differential in goals grew too humiliatingly great, we purposely scored two own goals to even things up. The visiting teacher, who was refereeing, was incensed by this communist subversion of the ethos of sport that ought to be the crucible of leadership and a metaphor for public service; he ranted to anyone who would listen that we were all immoral, corrupt and unnatural and did our parents know, and that he would never allow his boys to play against us again.

Being actively uncompetitive has remained with me. I can't bear games. Sports are ridiculous. I don't even like being part of a team. I can't care about cards, I don't like awards, I don't like the feeling that winning and losing impose on me. All for something that is essentially worthless, except as an allegory for something else that I don't believe in. I still trust that as a society we shouldn't sleep until everyone has a bed and that you can tell more about a nation by how it treats its lunatics than how it treats its footballers. And whilst the teaching was forgettable, there was the one, an English teacher, Peter Scupham, who didn't really teach English so much as uncover it. Exude it. Produce it like the world's greatest magic trick. He would come into the dormitory at night and sit by the window and read M. R. James ghost stories by the light of the moon. Late one night I was prowling around, visiting girls' dormitories, and I saw a light on in the English department. Gingerly I put my head round the door. Peter was sitting on the floor, surrounded by the dismembered corpses of *Two Gentlemen of Verona, Titus Andronicus, Troilus and Cressida*, all untimely ripped from thumbed and spavined school-edition Shakespeares. He was busy tearing them up, dozens of them. "What are you doing out of your bed . . . a bed?" he said without interest. "I suppose you're wondering what I'm doing? Once in

a while you've just got to show them who's boss." Peter ran—
or rather sauntered—away with Margaret, the games teacher.
They went to a small manor house in Norfolk and started a
press to print Chaucer, and he became a splendid antiquarian
book dealer and a considerable poet. Peter Scupham gave me
something far more lasting and useful and memorable than
exams or respect for nineteenth-century novels. He showed me
a man who plainly loved, and could shepherd, words with the
assured elegance of Cerberus, snapping the backs and tearing
the guts out of Bardery. It was a saving grace. A liberation from
the hallowed hushed reverence for books. The careful cradling
of them, the delicate turning of pages, the idolatry of paper
and the marching columns of little black glyphs that moved
and inverted and made nonsense and a fool of me. It was the
one moment of true education in a long and tedious scuffle
through school—nothing writ is holy, not even Holy Writ.

I've had a much happier relationship with books since then.
They know who's boss. Whenever I write one, I send it to
Peter. I hope he uses them to start fires. He started one for me.

Peter never mentioned dyslexia. In fact no one did. Saint
Christopher's had no real—or even unreal—idea of how to
teach those with learning difficulties. There was no cure and no
dedicated staff, no plan, no joined-up thought. Just a general
woolly belief in finding your inner spelling bee, helped by the
nice plump woman. The school may have sold my parents a
wishful lie, but essentially all schools that claimed to help alle-
viate or extinguish word blindness or innumeracy are still offering patent lies. Regimes that are about as efficacious as this

Sunday's fashionable diet: colored plastic sheets, spectacles, standing up instead of sitting down, phonetics, meditation, calisthenics, sweets, bribes, compliments . . . In the end it always comes down to the nice plump woman who sits with you and, in a kindly, prodding voice, suggests you try again . . . but concentrate this time. The plump lady is not there for the child's support, she is there for the school's, to show that they're on it. They're doing shit. Getting it fixed. Still, the medicine given to dyslexic children is more work, extra writing, remedial reading, more numbers . . . the utter abysmal useless cruelty of this has never occurred to a teacher. To compound failure with repeated failure reaffirms this humiliation and the fear and the loathing for words and learning, constantly pushing a door marked LUPL. You wouldn't treat any other condition like this. It has nothing to do with the difficulty or uniqueness of dyslexia. It is all about the inability of teachers to think outside their narrow one-way street of learning. "I say and show, you see and hear and learn." The answer to all learning difficulties is more teaching, and if the kids grow slow or contrary or surly, as they're bound to, then it's "more" more teaching.

Ironically, a dyslexic does learn. We learn a series of sleights and misdirections to get us through the misery of the special slow "try again" learning. I watched my son doing it. He relies on your impatience because, with the best will in the world, teachers, particularly kindly plump women, will encourage by offering hints, noises and vowel sounds. They can't stand the suspense or the fact that we can fail to recognize a word we managed a moment ago. The child learns to decipher these with a lightning speed then gets the word right or will rattle a stream of possibilities till he hears the squeak of congratulation that gives the teacher a little glow of pleasure, because she's taught well. The recognized word is her little success, and the dyslexic will continue to encourage the plump woman, will help and reward her with the right word and a big smile that looks like gratitude but is actually pity because we found someone who's worse at what they do than we are.

Essentially, a dyslexic child will cajole adults into reading for him; he will also listen to other children to learn content. My elder son can have knowledgeable conversations about the entire Harry Potter series without ever having read one, and both my boys have learned to radiate an ungainsayable, granite-melting charm that slides them through classes on casters made of flattery. None of this works with maths. I have worse dyscalculia than dyslexia. And the plump lady would sit and say, "Now, Adrian, if you go to a shop and buy something for fifteen shillings and sixpence . . ." What have I bought? "A hat, you've bought a hat . . . and you hand the shopkeeper a pound note. How much change will you get?" I'm sure it'll be the right change. "But how do you know?" Because it's a hat shop. He's a hat shopkeeper. They wouldn't let him near the till if he couldn't add up. And if he can't count, then he's just as likely to give me too much as too little. "But what if he's cheating you?" Well, *he* doesn't know I can't add up. It's a bit of a risk just for 15s and 6d.

I never understood or memorized the rules of mathematics. I can't do long division, or short division for that matter. The maths leading up to O Level was inexplicable. We still used log tables. Does anyone now know or care what a logarithm is? If you were late with homework, you would be made to work for an hour and three quarters on Saturday morning, like in *The Breakfast Club*. It was a big deal. Boarding school pleasures are scant and occasional, and Saturday mornings were when we were allowed into town (you can't get scanter than the occasional pleasures of Letchworth), and it was when your parents would visit. On Saturdays, we could go on bike rides on the Icknield Way. They'd put the list for Saturday study up on Friday and I was always on it. When I left school at seventeen without an exam or qualification, I was made to go and see a careers adviser in lieu of punishment for smoking. I asked him if I could become a careers adviser. "I don't think you're likely to be able to achieve that," he said, looking at my form. "Edited the school magazine, I see you're arty." He made the word sound like a synonym for sodomite. "I would suggest you consider training to be a hairdresser."

Mr. King-Harris, with his unexamined bluff self-confidence and glacial smile still intact, shook my hand and wished me luck in whatever I decided to do next. "I'm not sure we were always a perfect fit," he said, thinking about his dovetails. "We've never had a pupil who has been put on Saturday study as often as you." He beamed as if it had been a shared hardship. Every single Saturday for seven years. And I thought as he gripped my hand that it was an ignominious proof of the inflexible self-interest that runs through teaching and teachers, like the illegible writing through sticky seaside rock. Whose failure, Mr. King-Harris, does that represent, yours or mine? It's a rhetorical question. He is long dead, run over by a lorry whilst on a cycling holiday on Gozo. It will have been his right of way, right up to the very end.

I went to assembly for the last time and sang "Jerusalem," the school hymn . . . for the last time . . . and blubbed. Boarding schools are miserable, twisted and maladjusted institutions made weird by generations of miserable twisted and maladjusted people who fashion them into simulacrums of their own gimpy insecurities and fill them with children who are sent away for a farrago of reasons that are mostly about their parents' projections, aspirations, failures, fears, snobbery, vanity or simply a lack of imagination. I think my parents' reasons were decent and caring. Their aspiration was all for my good and the fear of what would be lost without education. I shared dormitories with a disproportionate number of boys from divorced families, too many from homes that were abroad, and the saddest child I've ever known, Suleem, an East African Indian whose father owned bakeries in Dar es Salaam. He was spindly and spectacled and shy, with beautiful deferential manners. Consequently he was friendless and periodically, thoughtlessly, picked on, but mostly, more cruelly, ignored. Deftly lonely, he would walk around the school like a chilly ghost, and I would find him at weekends on his bed, sobbing, looking at photographs of his brothers and sisters. My overriding memory of school was of a terrible, yawning, relentless boredom, the sluggish hours between bells and petty institutional routine. But there were also inevitably good things . . .

always things that were despite the institution, not because of it. My bike. Good mates. Big laughs. Canned Heat, The Doors, Cream. I'm surprised to remember how serious we were about politics, Vietnam, feminism, human rights. I joined the first Amnesty group, and there were books—I could read, just slowly, and consequently my comprehension is very good. I had a titanic crush on George Orwell, and Albert Camus, Mervyn Peake and the discovery of poetry. First through the Great War, but quickly on to Eliot, Larkin, Heaney, the Liverpool poets, Ted Hughes and the bleak flintiness of *Crow*, and by a small step to *The Bell Jar*, because every girl over sixteen said she couldn't love a man who didn't love Sylvia Plath or Carole King, and I must have undone bras to every track of *Tapestry*. And then there was the drink and the drugs. I remember with a Proustian wonder my first acid trip, which went on for hours in the summer sun like a brilliant cartoon. I stood on a hill laughing and throwing iridescent wine gums at passing air-planes. They ascended like sparkling comets. I sucked hollow-cheeked at massive joints of Red Leb and sticky Moroccan Black and opiated dope from Afghanistan. We smoked Gitanes and Sovereign and shared No. 6, walking through moonlit fields, swigging cooking sherry in evening hedges. The nearest pub was two miles away in a village called Willian, where The Fox would serve underage boys bottles of beer out of a back window and we would sit in the graveyard of the old church and giggle and snog and undo bras and roll back pretending to be drunk, herding cows onto the immaculate cricket table. I liked sidling through the front gardens of the little suburban cul-de-sacs in the dawn, pulling the heads off roses to fill my jersey with petals and cast them over a sleeping girl and then watch her face as she came down to breakfast in the morning.

On my last Saturday, I lay in the familiar sweet fields with an assistant matron who was blond and bored and gamine with a provocative pink pout. She was older than me and she lay on top of me and held my face and whispered into my mouth, "You're so new, so pleased with yourself, have a big life, I'll never see you again."

Boarding schools dip you in an unfading nostalgia; like the Venetian sea snail purple, it gets deeper and lustrous the more you try to wash it away. The core, prime, defining purpose of public schools is the self-preservation of the institution. Children and curricula are merely the means to that end. All the high-minded selfless Mr. Chippery is delusion and promotion. Childhood is the fuel flung into the furnace that school was run on. They need to make sure you are contagious enough to infect your infants.

When Flora and Ali were born, I repeated the oath I'd muttered on my first bunk. Ali was dyslexic in the same way I was, he struggled at school and grew to be a past master of the alternative parallel learning of avoidance and charm, the dyslexic's craft, far harder and more profoundly valuable than anything that's book-learned. Flora was diligent and did well, she liked school and liked being praised. Then, when she turned thirteen, she said, "Dad, you know you said you would never send us away, well, I've been to see a school that I really like . . . and I've had an interview and they've said I can go, but it's a boarding school. Will you let me?" And so I let her. And a year later her brother followed, and they loved it. It was a school not unlike St. Christopher's. I spent my time in the art room because that's where dyslexics go, to paint, or the pottery shed, the carpentry workshop, the dance studio, the music room. These are the corners of academe that don't deal in letters and numbers. When dyslexia became the chic children's condition, along with outré intolerances and something-or-other up a spectrum, mothers would gush, "Oh, you've got it? So has my little Noah. He's artistic too." There's absolutely no evidence that dyslexics are more innately prone to artistry than those who can do crosswords and work out percentages in their heads, it's just that we practice. On the principle that ten thousand hours makes you master of anything, we put in the time avoiding the columns of black squiggles.

The muse I really wanted to be kissed by was Clio. My passion was history. I loved it. It was the only subject I worked hard at. Our history teacher, Gammy Mercer, a malevolent, bitterly mean man with a withered hand, wasn't a good teacher. He wasn't even a good human, too busy being resentful about his own sorry life. But still I worked hard and he consistently marked my homework as failed. After a couple of years, I was upset and disheartened enough to stay behind and ask him— not an easy thing, he didn't like pupils and was terse and sarcastic—Why do you mark me so badly? I know my history is better than this. "Your history? Oh, your history. Yes, you're one of the best in the class at history. I'm marking you the way an examiner will. You have a problem with your writing," and he walked off. I thought, Actually, you know, I don't have a problem with my writing . . . you've got a problem with my writing. Fuck you. I'm never going to let this be my problem ever again. And I never have. I've always made it someone else's.

This book isn't written by me, it's written by Michelle. She's typing it now. It's getting late, I'm in my little study in the corner of my kitchen reading this from unpunctuated, ungrammatical type on a screen. If I leave it for more than a couple of weeks, even I can't read most of it. The computer is an *aide-mémoire*. Why don't I use a spell check? Well, the computer can't read my writing, either, and voice recognition stops you writing altogether, it's just moaning out loud. Writing isn't joined-up chat. It isn't recorded speech. There is a particular process, a connection between brain and hand that is very similar to drawing. I speak it into the phone. Michelle is sitting in her kitchen with chickens . . . I can hear the chickens. We've been working together for a long time. She's very accurate, very fast . . . used to be a copytaker on the paper when they still had copytakers, who would famously be tersely unimpressed by journalism: "Is there much more of this?" they'd say, in the middle of a deathless paragraph from some hellish danger zone. Then they let them go because everyone files on their computers—except me. Michelle and I kept going. I don't know how many books and articles and words she's plucked out of the air and made solid. We've known each other for a lot of years now, but we've never actually met. Talking to her in the quiet evenings has been one of the most enduring pleasures of my life with words . . . and now I can tell she's blushing.

I never really understood how angry I was about the dyslexia thing until I went to write a story about it for *The Sunday Times Magazine*. I hadn't written about it before, not because I wanted to keep it secret or was ashamed, I just didn't want to be known for it. I'd had enough worried mothers bearding me at parties. My line was that it wasn't that big a deal; it's only a big deal at school, but that's the school's problem. When you leave, you never think about it again. I can't remember a single time in my life when dyslexia has stopped me doing something. I can't fill in online forms with confidence, but it just stops me buying shit I don't need. I can't read an ordnance survey map, either, but I've never been lost in a wilderness. I had a thing I used to say to parents who'd want me to tell them the secret, what to do with their children who are failing to read and write. I'd lower my voice and say, "Look, between you and me, I can fix this . . . like, I can cure it. There's a thing I can do. I don't tell everyone of course, I'd end up having to do it all the time, but I can cure Noah now. No pills, no spectacles, no meditation . . . I can just do it. But there's a cost. There is always a consequence. He'll be able to spell like a dictionary and add up like a bookie . . . but he'll be ugly. So is that okay? He'll be quite ugly. As ugly as he is dyslexic, so do you want me to go ahead?" Of course no, obviously not. But that's the perspective, that's how important dyslexia is, cosmetic skin-deep. It's other people's problem.

When I was preparing to do the story, I spoke to an academic. The country's leading authority on learning difficulties. He said that dyslexia didn't really exist. We spoke for an hour and I was convinced. He pointed out that no single condition can have as many disparate symptoms as dyslexia has been given—everything from short-term memory loss to having an untidy room to not being able to tie your shoelaces or catch a ball—that's not to say that word blindness is imaginary or middle-class stupidity, it's just that it's a learning difficulty along with lots of other things that can make learning difficult. But the name got some traction. It was a label that caught attention, it made teachers listen, and local authorities are bound by statute to make provision for it (a plump lady). And so it's a lifeboat for desperate, disappointed parents with all sorts of children who aren't achieving what their parents want them to achieve. Dyslexia has become an ark for so many fears and worries, full of wide-eyed little Noahs, frightened and guilty—not about reading or writing, but about constantly disappointing and upsetting their parents. So I went to visit a special school that treated dyslexics to get them through common entrance so that they could go on to boarding school. It is a well-meaning place run by nice, decent, kind and committed teachers. I sat in on a maths class with nine-year-olds. There were only five of us, with a teacher half my age who gave us all a packet of sweets, and we were told to sort them into columns and percentages and I didn't know what he was talking about. And the most unexpected thing happened: I felt a flooding panic that was such a strong recall of incomprehension and fear. A feeling I hadn't had for forty years. It burst out of the cave I'd bricked it up in with insouciance. I thought I was going to sob, and the little girl beside me sensed it, because we are sensitive to each other, and she did my sum for me and smiled at me.

The headmistress asked if I would mind talking to the children at assembly, just a few words about how I'd coped with—"overcome," I think, was the word she used—my dyslexia. How long do you want me to talk for? Oh, about twenty minutes should be fine. God. We strode into the gym and there were the children sitting in neat lines and the teachers around the walls like prison guards. The headmistress introduced me and I stared at the rows of faces and I recognized every one of them—the look that is half open, half closed, inquisitive and guarded—and the great, hot spike of anger rose from the pit of my stomach. I felt light, a little unhinged by the shock and the ancient familiarity of it, all those childhood years spent being patronized and patted, blamed and resented and excused. The years of being a problem, a down beat, a blot on the graph, a glitch in the table. I opened my mouth and let the spike go.

"This is only for the children here. We're dyslexic, but there's something you need to know. Something they don't tell you, we have to learn it for ourselves. This language in your mouth, the words that don't need spelling in your head, this English, is the greatest thing that biology, civilization and natural selection have got to offer. Nothing else in a hundred thousand years has come close. It is the finest language ever coined. Not just by a little bit, not just by a couple of commas and a simile, but by volumes, by torrents of words, of meaning, of metaphors, of allegories and parables, of such nimble perspicacity, so exact and specific it can encompass a universe and split an atom. It is bigger than every god ever imagined. It is a thing not just of unparalleled power and accuracy but of peerless beauty and elegance. Heartbreaking poignancy and breath-catching loveliness. It is sinewy, gutsy, ballsy and bowelsy, shitty, pissy, bloody and snotty. It is heroic and mythic, has the strength to crack worlds, and is as delicate and subtle as dew on a web. All other tongues huff and puff in its wake, nothing has its poise, no other language comes close to English in its vista or its vision and it's yours, all of it, every single syllable and long hallooed vowel, yours for free, yours for life. If you have English in your head, you can already think things that people who don't have it don't even know they can't think . . . and no one can take it away from you, no one has more right to it than you do, no one can tell you what to say or how to say it, there are no rules, no lines, no instructions to this English, there is no correct accent or pronunciation, no proper order or style, it doesn't have judges or a police force or governors, you can't be punished for getting it wrong, because there is no wrong. Dictionaries don't police language, they chase along behind it. Grammar is whatever suits your design and need, there are no commandments of grammar, only people too frightened of its power with small, clogged and clotted minds. Teachers don't give you the language and their marks are mean-ingless, they don't have the keys to it or the secret of it, it wasn't made by a committee or a common room or a club, it was built by people like us, millions of them, not in classrooms or halls or palaces or churches, but in streets and fields, in trenches, at sea, in forests and tundra, in jungles and on top of mountains. In shops and stinking laboratories, in barracks and hovels and tents and gibbets and stiles, in ditches and over garden walls, in cradles and in dreams. It is the one truly, wholly democratic free and limitless thing we all own, it is yours. It will do whatever you ask it to do, in as many ways as you can imagine saying it. Don't ever, ever allow anyone to use this language against you, to make you feel excused or silenced or small or to make you doubt that you own every single breath and sign of English, and never speak it like a guest with an apology or deference or hesitation. Dyslexia is only one word. It is our word. There are millions of other words and they are also all our words."

And then, I was lost for words. The spike of anger evaporated. I stopped and there was an English silence, and all those unmade faces.

THERE'S A GLASS CABINET in the house I now live in with Nicola and the twins. It's an old shop fitting, probably a vitrine from a haberdasher's or a chemist's. I put things in it, curiosities. Things that don't go anywhere else. There's a blue whale's cochlea; the kneecaps of a medieval child; a pair of spectacles with a false nose for the *mutilé de guerre*; my grandfather's First War dog tags; a stuffed hoopoe; a pre-Columbian quern stone; a piece of fool's gold from eGoli; two finches preserved in salt from the Kalahari; a model of heroic communist women from Tashkent; a collection of weaverbird nests; Dark Age teeth in fragments of jawbone; Haitian voodoo dolls, one black, one red, and one half black and half white for mulattos, with real head and pubic hair; a small, probably European, probably Bronze Age, fertility figure that I gave to Nicola before the twins were born; Zuni Indian animal fetishes; Greenland whalebone tupilak carvings, part seal, part man, part fish; a toothless human skull given to me by Damien Hirst; Roman coins from Carthage that my father bought from a hissing Berber behind a Doric pillar; the bullet I shot a buffalo with; a bullet from Gettysburg; a stuffed ruff; a Bushman's bow and quiver; an Ethiopian royal guard's headdress made from a gelada baboon; a plastic model of Sigmund Freud with a Japanese manga schoolgirl; a rabbit's scut; a small dinosaur's coprolite poo—and that's not the half of it. I spend a lot of time staring into the cabinet. It is a mirror. A slowly accumulated self-portrait, a simulacrum of the inside of my head—an incoherent, crowded, Gadarene collection of artifacts, each of which launches a story or an anecdote that leads to another and another, but none of them having any real intellectual or scientific rigor or purpose. Alone they are just objects of votive or squeamish interest, like the ivory-faced Victorian hemorrhoid clamp. This isn't a case that tells you anything profound about the objects themselves or their place in the world. There is no historic or philosophic curation, no bigger picture, no encompassing question. It is the antithesis of scholarship, a magpie serendipitizing. Altogether it says something pathetically small and dormitory sad about me. Still, after all these decades, the need to prove that I'm not dim. They are the props for a character I don't really have—the tchotchke of an eighteenth-century reason, a broad Linnaean Aristotelian inquiry that isn't really there. It is merely a bowerbird's collection of shiny gewgaws, a clutter of insecurity, armor to deflect the blows of stupidity, the patronizing smiles of ineptitude, the muttering and tooth-sucking, head-shaking shoulder-shrugging disappointment of underachievement. It isn't a cabinet of curiosities, it's a memorial to a thousand disappointments.

Well, now I know lots of things. Lots and lots and lots and lots and lots of things. Lots of things about lots of things about bigger things—but they're not joined-up things. For as long as I can remember, I've stored away facts like a mad old muttering man clipping newspapers. The facts aren't useless in themselves, in the sense that words aren't useless, but they are purposeful only if they're combined into phrases and sentences. A solitary fact, a single unattached nugget of knowledge, is an orphaned Lego brick. For instance, I know that ducks, geese, swans, ostriches, flamingos and chickens all have penises— chickens only just. Most other birds don't, they have cloaca, which they rub together briefly in what's known sweetly as the "cloacal kiss" to pass on sperm. Do you think penis envy explains something about birds' behavior: all that shouting and screaming, the flocking and flapping, the eagle all talons and beak, mighty soaring emperor of the dawn, but nothing downstairs where it counts? But your pond duck, the joke inspiration for Daffy, Donald and bath toys, is out there dragging weed. In fact, the single largest penis of any vertebrate comparative to body length belongs to the Argentine blue-bill. Its curly duck dick uncoils for half its body length. Little wonder the blue-bill has to be afloat to get an erection. But the really interesting thing is that once all birds had penises. They evolved from dinosaurs. They owned great velociraptor knobs. So the real question is—why did they get rid of them? To lose a penis from one species is a misfortune, to lose it from a whole genus goes beyond careless, it's a fucking Darwinian-humping disaster. Imagine giving up your willy for evolutionary convenience.

The collecting of pub quiz information is an intellectually insecure nervous tic; the cerebral equivalent of nouveau riche overdressing for a golf club lunch. It's assuming a slightly posher accent—something else that I've acquired, along with bow ties. Only looking back from my "give a fuck" sixties do I see how much I minded, how hurt I was by being stupid. So I'm barnacled with this thick crust of facts. They are a menial weight, not ballast, just a Sisyphean resentment against my stammering, word-blind bottom-of-the-classness. So I'm sure that you know that the man who shot Abraham Lincoln was John Wilkes Booth . . . but I know that the man who shot John Wilkes Booth was Sergeant Thomas "Boston" Corbett. Shot him with his Colt pistol in the back of the head, almost exactly the same spot where Lincoln had been shot. Corbett was born in England and was a hatter by trade. Milliners used mercury for curing skin, it's a poison that affects the brain—hence Lewis Carroll's Mad Hatter. Corbett was definitely odd, he was exceedingly religious and castrated himself with a pair of scissors to prevent lust. He then had a spot of lunch before walking gingerly to hospital carrying his severed dick. Free as a bird from the tweet of carnal desire.

If you'd really wanted to know that, you could simply have picked up your phone. Carrying information around in your head is as pointlessly antediluvian as memorizing every phone number you'll ever need. It's like dressing up and sounding like someone you're not—the knowledge is off-the-peg imitation wisdom. Knowledge is not a synonym for clever. Clever is not in the same bed as wise. In fact, knowledgeable might be an indicator of a lack of wisdom. The problem with all this "Did you know?" baggage is that it's almost impossible not to use it. I can't stop myself. Last week I passed a statue in London and heard a tourist say to his wife, "I wonder what he did?" It was a rhetorical question. He assumed his wife didn't know and didn't care. He was commenting on the nature of statues and the passing off of fame rather than making an inquiry. In one half of my brain I knew that, but the other, vitrined half stuck its hand up and shouted, "I know, I know." I couldn't stop myself. "This is Napier of Magdala. A general dispatched to rescue Methodist missionaries held hostage in the impregnable fortress of Magdala in Ethiopia, or Abyssinia as it was then known, by King Tewodros II, or Theodore. After a staggeringly difficult march, Napier and his detachment defeated the emperor's army of nine thousand fanatical warriors with the loss of just two soldiers. Theodore shot himself with a revolver that had been given to him by Queen Victoria, having set fire to all his wives. Napier looted Ethiopia on behalf of civilization and the British Museum, returning home a national hero, and they put up this statue to him. He shouldn't be confused with another Napier, Charles James. He stands in Trafalgar Square. He too was in charge of an army, this time in India. He was instructed to subdue the troublesome Sikhs, but on no account to acquire any more land for the stretched Empire. He fought another glorious battle where sixteen dysentery-dribbling Highlanders and a jammed Maxim gun decimated a gazillion French-trained, well-disciplined Sikh warriors on the Plain of Sindh and contrarily accepted a vast new swath of territory for the crown. He sent back a telegram of a single word: '*Peccavi*,' which is Latin for 'I have sinned.' A pun that was printed in *Punch* and made everyone chuckle and feel warmly patriotic, because that's just the sort of élan and classically mocking savoir faire we expected from army officers standing up to their belt buckles in the gore and guts of dusky, fearsome natives whose land we were purloining. But I expect you probably already knew that. Everyone knows that. But what you may not know, what I do know [see how infuriating this becomes . . .], is the bonus fact that in fact he didn't send the telegram at all. It was a joke made up by a Mrs. Catherine Winkworth, who posted it to the magazine. And actually, you want to know about Mrs. Winkworth, for she was far nobler and more inspiring than either of the native-bashing Napiers. She was, by calling, a hymnist, who specialized in translating German hymns into English . . . and as *The Harvard University Hymn Book* points out, was more responsible than anyone for bringing German harmony to an English-speaking audience. Of far more lasting value than the dusty Plain of Sindh or some broken Coptic crosses in Bloomsbury. She was also a fervent proselytizer for women's rights, particularly education . . . She was on the board of Cheltenham Ladies' College—where, incidentally, my second wife went. There is a memorial to her in Bristol Cathedral and she is venerated by both the Evangelical Lutheran Church and the American Episcopalians, her feast days being July 1 and August 7, respectively."

Well, when I'd finished all that, I was talking only to Napier of Magdala, and he wasn't listening. This trainspotting pecksniffery, this faux-intellectual small talk, is one of the most unattractive and repelling social gambits and I'm stuck with it. The residue, the Plimsoll mark of miserably shallow and constantly disappointing schooling. I could tell you about Plimsoll and his mark, but I shan't. Let me instead draw the attention of your underfurnished craniums to Marilyn vos Savant, the blissfully apocryphally named possessor of the largest, highest, fattest IQ ever measured by Guinness World Records. A tome I can't be in the same room as. She came in at a massive 228. The mental equivalent of the Argentinian blue-bill duck dick—although this is disputed by people less intelligent than her. Marilyn took her globe-beating brilliance and turned it into the "Ask Marilyn" column of a popular American weekend magazine called *Parade*. Mostly she answers questions of probability. *Parade* has special issues throughout the year: "What People Earn," "Where America Lives" (under Canada, above Mexico, across the street from Russia) and "What

America Eats" (anything; everything). It also has a mission statement: "*Parade* celebrates the emotional touchstones of American life: We cherish family, friendship, the pride of small towns, and the rush of big cities. We champion good food and great writers. We believe in living longer, healthier—and happier. We adore holidays. We honor service. We delight in all types of personalities, from pop stars to presidents to favorite pets. We respect the past but live in the present. Above all else, we believe in America. We know who we are, and we're confident about where we're going."

What Marilyn is really doing with her IQ is living out a terrible cautionary tale of being too clever by half. If you ever wondered what too clever by half looked like, what the consequences of that disposable spittle-flecked schoolmaster's insult really were, there it is . . . being the problem page of *Parade* magazine. It is Marilyn vos Savant.

I'VE BEEN REREADING my father's autobiography, published just after he died, and I found this description of his RAF training barracks and the nicknames recruits from very different backgrounds and parts of the country gave to one another. "I rapidly became the Professor or Prof, though I think I was by a month the youngest in the squad. My years of enforced idleness had led me to read a great deal and I had information available on most subjects, knowledge I was only too ready to impart. Wyndham was better read, but a great deal more sophisticated in revealing it. Like all these epithets, mine was double-edged. It suggested learning, but also pedantry and an inability to cope with the practical side. A reputation well deserved."

ALL THAT TIME, for all those years, I wanted to be like my dad, to have him proud of me, and we both of us had the insecure curse of the English. I inherited the other half of the cleverness he had too much of.

9

Waking up was never the desirable option. Reentry into the corporeal wasn't orderly or smooth. It wasn't going into that good night—that wasn't the problem, sleep was a gentle glide, a peaceful anesthetic shutting down of function, like your dad going round the house turning the lights off, checking the windows. It was consciousness that I had to rage against. Sleep, though, was not an escape, not Morpheus's garden of blissful shades. The intrinsic problem of dreams, like holidays, is that you have to take yourself with you. Drunks' dreams are never a pretty, relaxed place. Mine came in two flavors—high anxiety and low anxiety. I'd be teetering on the top of a building, a cliff, a branch, a ladder, a mast, a gargoyle—anything that had a crumbling ledge or a trembling lip. Awake, I'm not particularly frightened of heights, but supine, unconsciously, I had hysterical vertigo. As children we used to say that you could fly in your dreams, but you could never actually fall, because, so the received ten-year-old's wisdom had it, the impact would be so traumatic it would kill you in real time. The dream would crash through the Freudian gauze between allegory and reality and, for a brief moment, your conscious and subconscious would become one. Your id and ego released into the tangible for a split second, you would be Schrödinger's dream—both completely alive and totally dead. I am born-again living proof that you can die nightly in your dreams. I'd teeter, then sway and jerk and scrabble and grasp and cry out and tumble into that hiss of weightless falling and the rush of the ground, the street, the water, the railings and then the enormous noise of the emergency stop. Terminal velocity hitting the immovably stationary dreamy earth, the twisting limbs, the numb promise of oncoming agony still falling. The pain catching up like thunder after lightning.

So, THAT WAS ONE DREAM. The other was that I'd lose the dog. Lily would slip her collar and run off, usually into traffic, or crowds, or a forbidding crepuscular landscape with a keening wind of foreboding. I would call and call and run after her and ask strangers to help, and unlike the fall, I would never find her, never get her back. So those were the two dreams. And I had one or the other every night in vivid, lifelike 3-D. Once I was startled awake by a death-fall and found that I'd landed next to a girl, almost on top of her. She was lying on her side, head propped on hand, watching me; she hadn't been there when I'd switched off and unplugged last night. She was the daughter of an ex-girlfriend who had come to my basement to . . . well, probably to upset her mother, and had found the door open as it always was, in case I had the dog dream. But the dog hadn't said anything and so she'd taken her clothes off and got into bed. "I couldn't wake you, nothing could wake you," she said, by way of explanation. "But you've been struggling and fighting and sobbing and muttering, and calling out. You kept calling for the dog and she'd thump her tail on the floor. You know she watches you all night? Of course you don't."

People have told me before that I'm hard to share the night with, but that wasn't the morning I meant to tell you about. The morning I'm thinking of, I'd pulled the emergency chain on sleep and slammed into the daylight with my head on the kitchen table. That in itself wasn't unusual. I woke up, my head on the sticky table, the radio chuntering, a streak of congealed thick blood smeared in front of me as if a desperate gory hand had gone to grab something—a knife perhaps—in self-defense or fury. And there was the knife. My own large French iron cooking knife, heavy as a rabbit, workmanlike as a machete. Mottled-gray ferrous metal that you could sharpen on the doorstep, its black handle thick with blood. I sat straight up, my ears filling with the terrible possibilities, the cold echo of an absent memory, a wiped tape, hands checking my face for gashes. The wall was spattered with matte maroon blood and not two inches from my face was the cold corpse. A grouse on a plate, surrounded by the traditional funeral ornaments of late August—bread sauce, fried bread crumbs, game chips, red currants, a bandolier of bacon, a sprig of watercress for modesty, a dish of congealed buttered cabbage. The floor was aflutter with feathers, evidence of a goblins' pillow fight. I had plainly plucked, drawn and cooked a grouse, made bread sauce by seething an onion studded with cloves and bay in milk, then added fresh bread crumbs and a scant teaspoon of dried mustard, white pepper not black, and salt . . . then fried more bread crumbs in goose fat and put them in the warm oven, peeled and turned waxy potatoes, slivered them fine (I didn't have a mandolin), dried them on a paper towel and shallow-fried them in yet more goose fat, sprinkled them with salt and a twist of black pepper, shredded a white cabbage, poached it with the diced end of pancetta, tossed it in a walnut of butter with a teaspoon of its own poaching water—the red currant jelly I must have bought in a bottle. And I'd done all this— knives, boiling fat, flaming hobs, ovens—dead drunk. In complete blackout. Too shit-faced to eat and too ill with alcoholic gastritis. But all that wasn't the weird thing, the mad thing. The spooky, unhinged bit was that I'd done it twice. There were two grouse, a brace, with their bread and tatties and cabbage. There was no one else here. Nobody expected . . . no one peckish for an early grouse likely to drop by. Who did I imagine I was feeding? Who was I propitiating? Was this a stuffed augury? Some hopeless offering to Bacchus or Pan or Loki? It wasn't the first time it had happened, I had come round to a Victoria sponge, gazpacho, numerous shoulders, legs and racks of lamb, and a tunnel-boned and forcemeat-stuffed chicken in a bain-marie. The only thing I'd forgotten about that was to turn on the oven—and then that I'd ever made it in the first place. It was discovered a week, or maybe two weeks, possibly a month later.

I DON'T KNOW when or why I became so absorbed with the alchemy of cooking. I know the story I tell, the quick anecdote. One day at college I'd realized I was spending an absurd amount of my beer money on food, but like most drunk students, I would eat only when hunger overwhelmed all the other pleasures, and when that happened I'd eat anything that was made: meaty, sweetie, salty, fatty stuff with a large bland hot blanket of carbohydrate—fried chicken, kebabs, noodles, pies, fish-and-chips, the milder curries. I'd eat till the moment ravenous became an appetite and then I'd give the rest to the dog. I reckoned I should be able to make something that would last all week and cost a fraction of a late-night takeaway. It didn't have to taste brilliant, just not be completely hospital food—how difficult could cooking be? People who couldn't do anything else did it.

After an afternoon's research into cost, ease of manufacture, availability of ingredients, number of utensils and storage, I came up with a rice pilaf thing. Actually more like *plov*, the staple dish of Central Asia, made with lamb, onion, carrot, a lot of garlic and cumin. It is an ancient dish that traveled with the Khans and their light cavalry from the Great Steppe as they became the most effective arbiters of power in the world for a couple of miserable centuries, thanks to stirrups and a psychotic collective id. As they conquered, leaving pyramids of skulls on the Central Asian plain, *plov* traveled and became pilaf and then pilau, having been refined by the Persians and the Afghans until it reached its elegant, delicate civilized apotheosis on the frontier in northern India and became the biryani of Hyderabad. I always thought the version I made was pretty coarse until many years later I ate it in Samarkand and Bukhara and found it was just as hick and thick as the Wandsworth version. In Uzbekistan, they prize the gobbets of opalescent fat from sheep's tails. Indeed, they breed special sheep with rotund, bulbous provocative swaying and twerking tails. The other dish was tuna flageolets, the simple Italian salad with pale beans, onions and tinned tuna with an olive oil dressing. This is best made with very good, carefully poached beans, pale Mediterranean tuna and strong peppery olive oil, but it's also perfectly moreish if brought together with the cheapest tinned beans, watery beige tuna and any oil that doesn't actually come from a toolbox. It gets better over a day and remains perfectly edible for a week in the fridge. I ate these two things a lot, and tripe and onion—brown honeycomb tripe poached in milk with chopped white onions, salt and pepper, thickened with flour and a dab of butter, eaten with mashed potato, beautifully pale and bland. There was something about the business, the process of preparing food, that I found comforting, not in a greedy, finger-licking way, but the procedural business of making. The mechanics of food, the sort of coloring-in-without-going-over-the-lines satisfaction of crimping pastry, the simple progression of cakes and pies, puddings and soups. But one thing led to another, the mechanical skills were pleasing and calming, the repetition of action—chipping, folding, peeling, plucking, popping, gutting, boning and rolling—metronomic, predictable, psyche-rocking jobs. People had done these things for generations, for thousands of years. There are few occupations as plainly worthy, as good, as uncomplicatedly worthwhile, as shelling peas or peeling broad beans or clarifying stock. You join a tradition, something wholesome and decent, that is older than the nation-state. For me it was in stark contrast to the constant Catherine wheel of counterconvivial chaos and failure; the alarm of shrill depression. I liked the being of cookery. The moment, lost in simple actions. I began to buy cookery books from charity shops, the detritus of house-cleared kitchens from the shelves of the dead. There was something touching about them, the stains and the smears and dog-ears; they would fall open at favorite recipes and special occasions. Simnel cake, made every Easter. The repetition remembered in the page just as the recipe was forgotten each Ascension Day and had to be relearned. The marginalia: "Use Apricot instead," "Doesn't work!" "Send to Trevor, Auckland." And caramel-yellow crisp recipes ripped from papers and magazines for celebrity canapés and things to do with leftovers. I'd find photographs of picnics and birthdays, the label from a champagne bottle that had commemorated something so memorable and so utterly forgotten, and once a letter from a wife: "I can't go on like this . . . I'm leaving you . . . Don't try and find me . . . I don't want anything from you . . . I wish you well, thanks for everything . . . This is the recipe for your Toad in the Hole." He had kept the letter, not as a terrible reminder of departed love, but for the recipe. The comforting taste of love. Pushed into a copy of Mrs. Beeton. Cookery books are the unconsidered diaries of family life, the everyday history of our civilization. Secular, earthly, holy books. The Torah of breakfast, the Veda of lunch, the Decalogue of dinner. And one thing led, as it inevitably does, to another. I began to acquire old bits of kitchen equipment, mangles and plastic egg coddlers, slicers and separators and timers, a singular apostle spoon, measuring cups, mixing bowls, the lost and discarded archaeology of family life, the Scotch spurtle that had stirred marriage, stirred the children to school, stirred retirement and bereavement. The cut-crystal liqueur glasses used for birthdays and Christmas to toast promotions and absent friends, the cruet set brought back from honeymoon that sat on a dresser for a lifetime, too silly to use, too fond to throw away, still with the grains of salt that had rested there, the symbol of a friendship and hospitality. A bread knife and board, the knife handle smooth from the palm, the serrated edge as dull as a spoon, the round board striped with the relentless measured thankful scars of a home: the morning toast, doorstop sandwiches for packed lunches and school trips, bread—the staple foundation of our lives for ten thousand years. Bertolt Brecht said there was real beauty in the worn tools of the craftsman, the dent in the workbench where the hammer is replaced after every repeated skillful blow that shines with as much intrinsic aesthetic value as the marquetry in a palace occasional table, or the bravura stroke of light in the corner of a gilded portrait's eye, or the final chord of a symphony. In the dying, shaming, unhappiness of my drinking, something kindred and pitiful, something about all this worn-out unconsidered kitchen equipment, the boxes of stuff shoved under secondhand-shop shelves of old shoes and board games and videos, everything 50p, touched me. They were imbued with as much mystery and votive power as Middle Kingdom funerary objects or the grave gifts of Mayans and Vikings. They were familiar and had no value, but their leftover stumbling, blunted, chipped and practical use was also noble in its exhausted simplicity. They'd fed families, sustained homes through good and ill, they were the evidence of lives that I would never be able to live. Now I understood; I am not unaware that this is all a heightened, operatic, maudlin and neurotic way to approach a pair of cracked bamboo salad tossers. I'm perfectly aware the projection was all mine in offering these pathetic bits of wood and china an agape, a pity and a dignity that I couldn't, didn't, offer myself.

If you ask anyone who collects or has a particular obsessive, repetitive open-ended interest in the specific, why they started, more often than not they will offer a story of quaint serendipity. A curiosity poked by a random encounter, a gift, a discovery in a junk shop, the tuna and beans, a discounted cookbook. This is disingenuous. Almost always a phony alibi. The truths of collections and obsessions are so fundamentally sensitive, they are too tearfully childlike to say out loud. I don't have to look far to see where my overly emotional reaction to food came from. It was Nick. It was all about Nick. I don't often talk about Nick, my younger brother. I don't ever talk about Nick. I don't know what to say. I avoid saying his name out loud. Nick disappeared, vanished, years ago. I don't know how many years ago now, but I'm waiting for a call, a knock. When I go to a new city, I search the streets for him. I look at things and stuff and views, but I'm also looking for him. Would I still recognize him? He'd be fifty-eight now. When I think about Nick, he's always just in his twenties. The last time he came to see me, he'd been having a furrowed time of it; angry, resentful. His ambitious single-minded life had been shredded. He came to my flat and we sat and talked in a way we hadn't since we were boys, about old things, soft gentle things, our childhood holidays, Paris, girlfriends, brother stuff. Then he stood up and said, "I could do with some money." I gave him what I had, seventy pounds, and a tweed shooting coat I'd just bought: it was cold. He got to the door and said, "I'm going away now. France maybe. But I'm not coming back." Well, don't just disappear I said, give us a ring. Let me know where you are. He smiled. He had a lopsided smile he used to deflect. We hugged. I think I said I loved him. I hope I did. And that was the last of him. Nothing. Not a hint, not a trace, not a court record, a hospital, not a Salvation Army bed, not a bank account, a credit card, not a passport, not a headstone. Recently our mother asked if I thought he was dead. "He's probably dead," she said. I understand. It's a hypothetical fork—the dead you can mourn; abandonment is a choice that's made every day. All those days deciding that today I won't tell my family I'm okay, or not okay . . . or alive. With the sadness there is also the throb of anger—I'm furious with Nick. The selfishness, the banked heat of his resentment. My father dying without ever knowing what happened to his son. Our mother. His kids. But there is also a voice that whispers: everyone has a right to chuck in the hand he's been dealt and get a new one if it becomes unendurable, unbearable. The penultimate option is to start again. I got that when I stopped taking the drugs. I stepped back into the world knowing that everything I did before had led me to this point, and that everything I did from now on had to lead away from this place, that repeating the past smarter or cuter wasn't going to do it, that experience isn't always the great teacher. Sometimes, mostly, it's just experience that you could have done without. I understand all that about Nick, but I thought that after a year or two he'd be better, happier, and he'd call to show off a little. Look what I did without you. And to square the past, to put it to bed. But mostly I think he'll call because he still misses me.

THE YEAR I WAS SENT to school we moved out—rather the rest of the family moved, sold the garden, rented a flat above Lloyds Bank on Kensington High Street. I came home from the holidays and discovered that strange otherness that boarding school awards to your home. You belong, but you don't really fit in. They treat you differently, with excessive interest, like you're a new piece of furniture. It's awkward. It was hard for Nick. And the flat brought a new sort of life. It was soon full of actors on sofas and sleeping bags. My room was let to a succession of lodgers, and when I came home I had to fight for a chair or a couch with the cast of whatever fringe play my mother was in. Meals were chaotic, noisy, competitive and histrionic, would drift one into the next. And then one day, our mother came into the kitchen and said, "I'm not cooking anymore," and that was it, she didn't.

My father would leave twenty pounds on the kitchen table every Friday and disappear, and I would shop—I was a frugal quartermaster, shaving enough for beer and fags—and Nick would cook. He must have been thirteen. It began with pancakes, he cooked a whole dinner party of different ones, savory and sweet crepes. Right from the beginning he cooked with a hunched intensity, a ferocious perfectionism. I have never seen someone fall with such ecstatic serendipity into a calling. Nick had never been a willing combatant in the family's intellectual scrum, he never read books, polished pretensions, he had nothing to say about French cinema or Florentine frescoes, he was comfortably earthbound. Food and Nick were made for each other. It is unnerving and compelling to watch someone expand into a craft that's so unexpected and unexplained. We all liked our food, but mostly as a cultural and social signifier, as a setting for conversation, intellectual communion. I was a vegetarian. Nick had found not just the thing he was good at, but the thing that would set him apart and set him free, that no one could criticize or argue or knew more about than him. The stove that my mother had thought chained her as a servant to the old patriarchal idea of a family liberated my brother from the family. But in three years he was better at his thing than any of us would ever be at ours, he had a fierce stubborn confidence and presence. He left school at fifteen and went to catering college. At sixteen, left home for Paris to work as a *commis-chef*. He spoke no French, knew no one there, lived in a cold-water walk-up garret, learned the hard ways of classic French cuisine. A kitchen is called a brigade because it is arranged like an army corps. The bullying and the discipline are unrelenting, designed to exclude and weed out the weak, the bruised and the imperfect. They treat champignons with more care than the staff. As an English boy with not even kitchen French, he was bullied and mocked relentlessly, burned, cut, snubbed. The list of cruel and painful practical jokes that *commis* have to endure is legendary. He worked split shifts, learned French in his break; laundering his whites cost half his wage. He told me that the proudest moment of his first year in Paris was when the dry cleaner, who had never acknowledged him, handed him back his neatly starched and folded uniform and called him Monsieur le Chef. Nick had no money, no friends, no sleep, but he had the respect of an eminent profession, in its capital city. One of the best moments of my life was going to visit him for a weekend with my father. It is the only time I can remember the three of us being together, and Nick was changed. Paris had been the city our dad had showed us; now it was Nick's. He walked with a square-shouldered insouciance, wore the stripes of his burns and scars with a shrugged pride. We stayed in a pension in the Rue de Buci above the market and one day on a whim we went to Longchamp for the races; we'd run out of money—this is before credit cards—and pooled thirty francs and put it all on a *plongeur*'s kitchen tip. The horse came home. But it wasn't really the nag that came home, it was Nick. So we took the winnings and went to La Coupole for dinner—the three of us, bright and happy, light-headed with the city and with the aura of Nick. We had *marc* and coffee, and Dad called for *l'addition*, pulling out our wedge. The manager bustled over, shook Nick's hand and tore up the bill. He bowed to my dad and said as Nick was a chef, it was a privilege to have this young man's family. He was now theirs, folded like egg white into the great tradition.

He went on to be one of the best, and the youngest, English chefs ever to get a Michelin star, and then he disappeared. My interest in cooking began as a way of being close to him, it was something we could talk about. There is no end to discussing food, and when my drinking got bad and I had a long summer of pitiful depression, I'd go and stay with him in Rutland and we'd swap places. He'd be the older brother and bring me back delicious and thoughtful late suppers and we'd go through cookbooks together. He was funny and fraternal and never asked how I was. Everything he knew—taste, texture, tem-perature, food—was the allegory of family. Life was merely the table that it came on.

I USED TO DRINK with a butcher called Butch. I'd pick him up as he finished work, hang out in the shop. He'd give me meat ends: stringy, slippery splintered things, slithery mottled and delicate things from the dark caverns of gut, snouts and lips, cheeks, tongues, brains, spleens, glands, lungs, feet, tails and ears. You need to clean a pig's ears. They're like humans, they have earwax. I got a bag of lamb testicles once, fries. These were still taut and terrified in their furry scrotums.

People who think about food when they're not hungry aren't normal, aren't balanced. They're not happy. What we're thinking about isn't food. Food is what we juxtapose when we can't look directly at the grief. Food is our safe word, our happy place. In all the years I've spent writing about the groceries, peeling them, traveling to meet them, I've come to understand that none of it is really about butter, eggs and sugar at all. Everybody I've met along the way who's been doing excessive, obsessive things to ingredients, making restaurants, working in kitchens, writing books—they're not happy. They weren't happy children. Nick wasn't happy. I wasn't happy. We're not compelled to examine kitchens by a Falstaffian appetite, we aren't the jolly trenchermen with a bonhomous desire to lay a better table. One of the great misconceptions about dinner is that nice people make good food. That there is a soul in honest, loving dishes that are passed from the hand of the chef to the mouth of a grateful diner, that you could trust a good cook. But it's almost exactly the opposite. Great food is cooked by twisted, miserable, depressive, cruel, abused and abusive, needy, compromised and shamed people. There is something in the pursuit of lunch that is therapeutic, allegorical, even redemptive. There is the pleasure of the business, the mechanics, the chemistry, the physics of food that soothes and calms. There is the transformation: that you take one thing and, through a series of votive actions, incantations, the application of fire and water and air, it becomes something else. In church at the altar, Catholics wonder at the transubstantiation of bread and wine into body and blood. Atheists sneer at this simple-minded delusion of faith, but none of them wonder at the equally miraculous transformation of flour and water into bread or spaghetti or a pancake or Yorkshire pudding or papier-mâché—how does it know? Or the ability of an egg to become mayonnaise, to go on and on and on transubstantiating a thin stream of oil into a thick emulsion, indefinitely. No one has discovered when a single yolk will get bored and run out of the will or the desire to transform oil. It could conceivably turn the oleaginous universe into a dip. Cooks are always a little unnerved and awed at the alchemy of cooking. You know it will happen, you've done it a hundred times, but still the revealed truth of meringue is a dainty relief. Making food out of earth and water and sunlight is a salutary blessing for those who have had their narrow lives made bitter and inedible, and the spell, the concoction, the offering of food is a wholly good thing from compromised hands. There is no part of it that is contaminated or equivocal or duplicitous. To feed someone is to make them, to wish them well, to add to their lives, to offer them warmth and comfort, well-being and hospitality. To give someone a diamond is to own them, decorate them, make them richer. But a baked potato gives them another day of life.

The bits of our brain that we use to judge and recognize food, our senses of smell and taste and appetite, are older than the bits of our head we use for language. They are the fundamental lobes we share with lizards, they are older than our humanity. You don't need to be able to understand or know the people you feed for the act of giving food to be completely understandable. We are the only mammal that can make eye contact and eat at the same time. For every other omnivorous or carnivorous species, communal eating is the most stressful, competitive and dangerous thing they do. It is at table that we prove our essential otherness. Where we reveal and recognize the spark of divinity. We can eat without hierarchy. Feed the neediest and weakest first. We have arrived at a set of manners that guarantees our safety and security whilst eating. We reserve the gravest odium for those who abuse the hospitality of the table.

The great leap in the growth of our species wasn't the taming and utilizing of fire—though you have to wonder at the bravery of the first hominid that dared to eat a well-done steak, it must have stunk of terror and death—but its benefit was enormous. It allowed us to eat much more, much faster. The fire made tough muscle and rubbery gut edible to young and ancient. It made it easier to share, it eliminated bacteria and parasites. But the real quantum leap wasn't the fire, it was the pot. The thumb pot, the coil pot. Turning mud into utensil— that's what allowed us to boil food. That is the bubbling birth of cookery. When you can put more than one ingredient into the pot, it is a recipe. And weaving, making baskets so that you can collect more groceries than you can hold in your hand, so you can prepare food to eat it later, you can plan ahead. And planning is what defines us. And pains us. Planning menus, making lists, is still the great orderly, calming pleasure, the psychic poultice. Then finally there is food as propitiation. I can't cook for one. I can barely cook for two . . . I have to cook for ten. I can't judge ingredients against mouths, there is a fear of not cooking enough. I'm always left with as much as I'd served—like the grouse, it's cooking for ghosts. There is, in making food, a repeating of the past: that every Sunday lunch will apologize for or make better the past Sundays, like the offering left on altars, the sacrifice and libation given to gods, I'm always feeding the ancient hunger of the past, the absent mouths. It's difficult to explain. You want to remake, to restore, the things that make you sad, to feed the loneliness, the stutter, the loss, the fear, the frustration. To satiate it, to soothe it, to make it all bread-and-butter better.

Eight years after I got sober, I was married again, to Amber, who didn't cook. Didn't need the therapy. Didn't have to bake the four-and-twenty black thoughts into a pie, had better things to do with her time than make lists of roots. She was starting a company. I was happy to stay home, to draw and write and cook. We had a baby daughter. One Sunday lunch, an old friend of hers who had just got engaged complained that her prospective mother-in-law was offering to send her to a cookery school so she'd be able to feed her son in the manner to which he'd been brought up to expect. "Take the money and go to Paris for a long weekend and never invite her to dinner," I said. Amber, being more practical, suggested I could teach her to cook, and so started the black dog cookery classes. I came up with a ten-week course. Nick had told me that people—particularly men—

are put off cooking because the ingredients and the quantum possibilities of combinations seem so daunting, like learning how to be a chemist in the evenings. And men hate being made to feel dumb in front of women. But what you should teach instead are the methods of cooking. There are only a handful of ways to cook anything—fry, grill, boil, poach, braise, roast, bake, acid, moisture, vibration. Once you've learned the fundamental physics and chemistry, the epicureanism is fun. The first lesson I called "What Is a Kitchen?" It was about kit. And what did you need and what does it do. Hands up who knows what the two most important bits of kitchen equipment are. They'd guess knives and ovens, pans and fridges. The answer is, a chair and a radio. You're going to spend a lot of time in this room.

I filled my kitchen with ingredients and people who said they wanted to cook for a variety of reasons—because they wanted to impress girls, feed their families, beguile their husband's boss, for a hobby . . . And we'd cook—all together. No one was allowed to write anything down, we never used recipes. You don't cook words, you cook ingredients. Mostly it was at least edible. Sometimes astonishing, occasionally laughable, like the attempt at spaghetti with chocolate sauce. I can still taste the lamb cooked in hay—one of the rare occasions when organic really makes a serious difference—you have to get hay that's untreated with pesticide. Best to go to a pet shop and ask for hamster bedding. And the dish I made up—lamb brains and oysters poached in ham stock and vermouth. We had an enthusiastic one-armed student who said she wanted to eat a foie gras omelet and she bought a beautiful goose liver. Glynn Christian, the food writer, was sitting in that evening. He said he'd have a go and made a brilliant risen omelet like a Swiss soufflé. I like risen omelets. You whisk the egg white and fold it into the mix, cook it on the hob and finish under the grill. It makes the best Arnold Bennett—an omelet invented at the Savoy for the critic who used to write his overnight reviews there and wanted something sustaining but not too heavy. It's made with smoked haddock, and if you add a light béchamel, a handful of grated Gruyère and a teaspoon of smoked paprika, it's a dish that has all the properties of an indecent proposal. We would make things that came with moral health warnings. There were dishes that I insisted you should make only for people you were prepared to go all the way with because it was unfair to lead them on with food that made promises you wouldn't honor. I told the boys that their kitchens were closer to their bedrooms than any restaurant—it was only partly facetious. You should never cook for people you don't like, but you should always cook for strangers, never for someone whose life you don't want to improve or wish well. Who you cook for is as important as what you cook. In the classes, we cooked for each other, and everybody could invite a friend, a partner, a date for eleven o'clock, and we'd eat whatever it was we'd come up with. They were some of the most engrossing and hilarious kitchen suppers. I discovered through teaching that I was a good cook. The distinction between a cook and a chef is that a chef does it for money, the cook does it for love. I also discovered through teaching that being a good cook isn't just about the quality of food you produce; that's plainly part of it, but it's in the making that cooks attain goodness. It's the pleasure, the relief and the absolution of allowing things to be greater than the sum of their parts. Sometimes what you end up with is miraculous, sometimes it's just edible, but cooking is constant, continuous, a lifelong occupation, as unending as the washing up. You may eat a chef's food once or twice; the cook's you eat every day. The goodness of the cook's craft is life.

What I cook and my commitment to the preparation of dinner changed when I had children. When Flora and Alasdair were born, I understood that what a cook makes isn't simply lunch and dinner. It is the lives that sit and eat. I know, I know, the constant comparisons between cooking and theology are awkward . . . No, they're eye-rollingly pretentious. Bottom line, food is a chemical and physical composting of sunlight into shit. It is basic and practical. A recipe isn't a philosophy, canapés aren't prayers or mantras, they're cheese biscuits. And food is fuel. At its most hoity, it is social decoration, and all the other stuff is just middle-class intellectualizing, overwrought twaddle, and of course that's perfectly correct. That is what food is as well. But it's everything else too. From salt-and-vinegar crisps to the body and blood of Christ, from mother's milk to your final sip of poppied morphine, food is the metaphor and the simile and the parable of every important moment in our lives. It is also at the heart of every religious observance. We pay the tolls of our love with cakes and champagne, cups of tea, and beans on toast.

One of the boyfriends who came to the cookery classes was a feature writer on *Tatler*, a social magazine. He asked if I could write six hundred words about my time in treatment. They were running a Good Rehab Guide. I wrote it and the new magazine editor liked it and asked me to come in for an interview. I'd never met a real editor before. Jane was exactly what I imagined. She took her earrings off to answer the phone. "I like that little piece you wrote. Would you do more?" Yes. "Would you do celebrity interviews?" What, ask people about their knicker drawers and if they'd slept with the gardener? No, I don't think I could do that. On a glossy magazine this is the top writing job and Jane raised her eyebrows like a flying buttress. "Well, what would you like to write?" Her voice was arched. Well, I noticed you don't have a cookery column. "A cookery column," she said. "Like a cross between Celia Johnson and Lady Bracknell? Most of our readers have no idea where their kitchens are—why would they want to read recipes? They're all on diets." Well, I said, no one thinks of food as much as someone who doesn't eat. And I could illustrate the column. "Okay," she said, "we'll take six and see how it goes." And she let out a laugh, like a string of pearls breaking into a urinal.

A year later I won the *Sunday Times* Magazine Columnist of the Year. The runner-up was a new gonzo motoring correspondent. Jeremy Clarkson and I have worked together on *The Sunday Times* for twenty-two years. He's godfather to my youngest son, and it still rankles him.

I WENT TO THE NAMIBIAN BORDER of Botswana to talk to the Bushmen about food. It was one of the most affecting and instructive things I've done. The Kalahari Bushmen are the oldest people on earth. We all have the same number of ancestors of course, about thirty ghosts each. For every living person there are, give or take, thirty dead ones. I find that quite comforting. Understandable. Manageable. The top deck of a bus of shades. The Bushmen are the oldest people who remain doing the thing they've always done in the place they've always done it. Very little happens to improve the Bushmen's life—iron, knitted hats, and the last big thing was tobacco. There is a seasonal water hole at Kia Kia that the archaeology seems to prove has been visited every year by the same families for thirty-five thousand years. Bushman DNA is surprisingly diverse. It was the rest of us that had to survive the bottlenecks of being economic migrants. They sing songs that have no words, they have titles— the song of spring; of rain; of new flowers—but their chanting refrains seem to have been made up and learned before spoken language. They might be the oldest cultural things on the planet. I wanted to hunt and gather with the Bushmen, because the old men and women still practice a tradition that is pre-agrarian, pre-pastoralist. This is where cooking begins. We went out trapping spring hares, sweet large-eyed little animals that look half wallaby, half hamster. The first one we caught, the hunter deftly snapped both its elegant thin back legs, which seemed unnecessarily cruel. And I pointed that out to him. He chuckled, a babble of clicks and singing vowels that translated as: The first rule of hunting is never catch anything twice. Men hunted, women painted their faces with red ocher and gathered. Gathering is twice as hard as hunting, but has half as many stories. The men would sit under trees smoking their ferociously dark tobacco, telling tales that were alternately filthy and merely dirty. Always funny. Whilst the women with their children on their backs took sticks and mined for roots and we all collected iridescent beetles that were delicious. When I first met the men in the chilly dawn, they were dressed in the hand-me-down charity detritus of the West and they came out and examined us with a curiosity of zoogoers and they offered us clicking names. Much easier than learning a new name in awkward English, they just gave us ones they made up. We were called things like "Lion That Sits," "Graceful Eland," "Flying Bustard." They got to me and clicked that my name was "Small Antelope's Shoulder Blade." Really? I can't pretend I didn't feel a little slighted. I've never really thought of myself as a small antelope's shoulder blade. When at the end of the day we returned to camp to make dinner, I was carrying a huge and repellent cannibalistic bullfrog the size of a Chihuahua in my pocket and the men took it to cook. They had a very interesting way of cooking, making a fire in the sand and then spreading it out, moving the sand and the embers so that the heat was regulated. Different things could be cooked at different temperatures. They talked and argued about it constantly. It was quite subtle. The bullfrog was bashed on its devil-eyed, smiling head and buried in the sand, the Bushmen flicked over the heat, moving the ashes and embers back and forth with a dexterously elegant spatula. Along with the digging stick, this was the essential kitchen utensil—probably the original kitchen utensil, older than the thumb pot. The great-great-great-great-grandmother of the lost and abandoned charity-shop spoons and knives.

The old man offered me the spatula and grinned. It was light and comfortable in the hand. "That's the shoulder blade of a small antelope, that's your name," he said. "We knew when we saw you."

Self-pity, the most undervalued emotion. No one admires self-pity, so universally derided it should feel sorry for itself. Go try to find a good word said in defense of solicitous self-interest—there isn't one. You'll come across more written in favor of fascism and sex with terriers than for inverted charity . . . it's defined as an ungallant weakness. People speak of self-pity in the way Victorians spoke of adolescent masturbation, a disgusting vice that led to moral feebleness and intellectual flabbiness. Self-pity is a solitary aberration—mortally embarrassing to be discovered practicing. The self-piteous are lonely, lachrymose, vain and neurotic specimens who self-massage their psychic onanism in the shameful dark; it is mental cranking—crying and wanking. Self-pity is so dissolutely disreputable that it has tainted the very idea of pity—don't pity me, spare me your pity. To be deemed pitiful is to be mortally insulted and dismissed, and in the eyes of the sober, self-pity is the defining weakness of the drunk. Drunks may begin to drink for fun, for life and soul, but then end up drinking through weakness, through lack of fiber and willpower. The social wisdom is that alcoholics and addicts are weak people and their real failing, their real moral delinquency, is self-pity. Every addict has heard variations on that theme, most often, most insistently, from people who love them, care about them, and whom they respect.

In thirty years of hanging around addicts, I have never, ever, found one—not a solitary one—who suffered from self-pity. In truth, it's usually quite the reverse. When I talk to drunks and junkies who are having a rough time, one of the first things I tell them to check is that they're not being their own most unforgiving critic. Whatever you think of an addict who is drunk again or stoned again, or gone AWOL yet again, failed to make it through a holiday, hold down a job, however deep your disappointment, it's nothing compared to theirs— the hellish and fierce recrimination they feel for themselves. Drunks' biggest tormentors are drunks. It's like waking up with a bully who knows all your weaknesses, all your guilty secrets, and every one of your delicate precious hopes. I've never met an addict who didn't join in with the chorus of criticism. It's not weakness that makes addicts feed their addiction, it's the addiction that keeps medicating the addicts weak. Actually, "weakness" is the wrong word. There was an old English pinstripe-and-tweed drunk I knew who got sober and admitted that he had no time for druggies' slovenly ways, until he listened to one describe his day and then he did a bit of accounting. What the chap needed to feed his habit, the amount of income that had to be generated every year, was, he discovered, a frankly staggering figure to get hold of entirely outside the system without any legitimate or expert assistance, without training or marketable skill, whilst being ill most of the time. He said, "I thought, that's an astonishing entrepreneurship. I'd go a long way to recruit people who had the work ethic and ingenuity of junkies." Addicts could do with self-pity. Any pity. The ability to see your own frailty and threadbare humanity. Pity doesn't absolve or excuse responsibility or accountability, it is a kindness and care. The character traits we're supposed to use to ward off self-pity—toughness, stoicism, endurance, willpower—are the least attractive in people. They bury and prolong unhappiness, and if you can't manage self-pity, then you should at least stop being your own vigilante.

As well as self-pity, the thing most people know about drunks and recovery is that everyone has a rock bottom . . . a decisive moment. It's how narratives and the stories of tragedy and redemption work: there needs to be catharsis. Some have them—a moment, a thing, a death, a prison sentence, a crash, an excommunication—but mostly they are recognized only in retrospect and are anecdotal. It doesn't feel like a single crisis after which there is understanding, acceptance and triumph. It's much more like running out of options, traveling desperately down a road that gets narrower and falls away till you're slipping and galloping just to stay upright . . . where the sides grow sheer and you can go no further, and you can't go back, and you can't go on, and each step, for a long time, has been decisive. The drunk's story often sounds like a Greek tragedy: preassigned catastrophes, the rock-bottom moment predicted right at the start as a foregone conclusion, chorused in sunshine and comfort.

But drunks tell stories that are different—of emblematic things that just happen. The Scotsman I was in treatment with lived in an east Glasgow housing estate. He bought a duckling from a man in a pub because he thought it would be a good thing to grow a duck for Christmas. He kept it in a canary cage on the balcony and fed it when he remembered. And talked to it, and drank with it . . . and come Christmas he remembered it was time to eat it, but he hadn't noticed or realized or he'd failed to comprehend that it was now wearing a cage like a straitjacket. He couldn't get it out. Another man told an old joke about two tramps sitting on a bench—the first one says, "You've shat yourself," and the other says, "No," and the first says, "There's a terrible smell of shite—you sure you haven't shat yourself?" "I haven't shat myself," says the second. "I don't believe you," says the first, "take your kecks off." The second tramp lowers his pants, and they're full of shit. "You said you hadn't shat yourself," shouts the first tramp. "I thought you meant today," replies the second. "That's a joke," the man said. And when I heard someone tell it in the pub, I thought, Fuck, how did he know? There was only me and Danny on the bench, and Danny's dead. Every drunk has a shitting-himself story. Alcoholic anecdotes are a scatology of inadvertently dropped turds, of walking home like John Wayne, a drunk's metaphysical fear of a fart and plosive diarrhea. I pissed bar stools, taxis, sofas and beds. The cringing humiliation of pissing someone else's bed when they're in it. I don't have a rock-bottom story . . . mine was a brick cul-de-sac. It was a doctor's waiting room. But there are things I turn into anecdotes for something to say and to remind myself. One is, I was drunk in Earls Court, on Earls Court Road. It was late at night, it was raining, I tripped and fell, straight forward onto my chin. I lay on the cold wet pavement. I remember it really clearly, the feeling of my cheek on the sodden stone, cold as the mortuary slab, the gentle rain, the relief of having collapsed, not having to stagger anymore, the reflective moon in the slick, the sound of wheels in the wet. Someone, a man, leaned over me and said, "Are you all right?" I mumbled to leave me alone. Soaking and bleeding on the pavement in the rain seemed like the preferable option, all things considered. I can still feel the little chip out of my chin . . . And then there was Londonderry.

My American cousin Wendy, the photographer who likes to organize cross-party photography in conflict zones, thought that Northern Ireland would be fun and inspirational, and she asked me to go with her on a recce. This was the '80s, it was particularly murderous there—a lot of bombs, a lot of shooting, a lot of intimidation and people in prison, a lot of groundbreaking kneecap-replacement work done at the Royal Infirmary and not yet an inkling of a peace deal. So I said sure. We went to Dublin just to have a look. I can't remember a thing about Dublin, just the taste of Guinness and Bushmills, and we took the train to Londonderry, got out at the station and asked the taxi driver to take us to the address she'd got. He looked at the paper and said, "Lucky you got the right sort of driver, the other sort wouldn't take you here." Which sort are you? I asked. "The Republican sort," he said, smiling. The photography club who said they would be happy to put us up and offer assistance turned out to be a Sinn Féin front for collecting money, and the family who ran it were as close to being IRA as you could be without having shamrocks tattooed on your forehead. It was an uncountable number of brothers, I was never quite sure how many because some of them were in prison and some on the run, and there was a mother who was a head-splitting gobby woman forbidden from entering the mainland and a poor father who was a silent mousy postman. The sons all had lists of convictions for all sorts of political violence, including attempted murder of a policeman. But apart from all that, they were warm, funny, hospitable, garrulous and catastrophically terrifying. They showed us round the city, pointing out martyrs on every street corner, and it was all fine until Sunday night when I said, Let's go and get a drink. And the boys said, "No, we'll stay in," and I said, No, no . . . we'll go and get a drink . . . And as none of them had a job, I said, I'm paying. Actually, Wendy was paying. And they said, it wasn't that, it was that you couldn't get a drink on Sunday—this was like Scotland, teetotal for the Lord . . . And I can still taste the rising cold panic. I couldn't . . . simply couldn't . . . go a whole night without a drink. I never had, not for years. I organized my intake, I knew what I needed, I couldn't sit in this tiny terraced house with the hit-squad boyos listening to Val Doonican, slowly getting the shakes and swallowing panic. No, no . . . we've *got* to be able to get a drink somewhere, I said. How close is the border? Now they were embarrassed and dogmatic, and then one of them said, "Oh, for pity's sake, there's the club . . . ," and the others said, "No, no . . . there's no club," but I was on the club like a terrier with a duck in a canary cage. Yes, the club, let's do the club . . . a club would be just the thing. And I went on and on like a child who has forgotten his Ritalin. Finally they said, "Okay, we'll see if the club's open . . . but it's not a good idea . . . Keep your mouth shut." And with as much ill-grace as they could muster and the brazen embarrassment of Wendy, we walked through the jolly evening drizzle of Derry. It was as if there was a voluntary curfew—no one was out. We traipsed across an inimically lit wasteland of ruin, and finally, through a deserted crepuscular alley, out of an unmarked doorway, a man, or rather the barely defined silhouette of a man with a turned-up collar and a broad-brimmed hat, appeared. It was exactly the cover of a noir nouvelle about the Troubles, and I would have laughed if I hadn't been so desperate. The brothers mumbled something and the man stood aside and the door let out a secret smear of light. We trooped upstairs to an empty room of trestle tables, chairs and a hatch in the wall that served as a bar, and I went to get in the pint of Guinness and the shots and I necked a couple as I waited for the barman to pour the beer . . . and I can still taste the relief. The cauterizing of the panic with the stinging spirit. It is as pleasurable as any feeling I can directly attribute to alcohol. We sat back at the long table and the room began to fill up with hard men.

I've been in rooms with tough bastards all over the world: mercenaries, military, terrorists, religious maniacs—but this was special. Everyone got a brief whispered biography . . . Five years in Long Kesh on remand; suspect; bomb-making; grievous bodily harm—you don't want to go crossing him, he's banned . . . and you never saw him. I'd be introduced, or rather explained, and I'd get the stare from under those bony, hirsute brows and they'd sit with their pint and polish their ancient grievances and they'd start telling stories and pretty soon they were singing them . . . and I'd get up and get in more drinks and listen as they chatted over blood and earth and chanted those Paddy ballads of sentiment, vengeance and unrequited nationhood with the verses that start in the Pale and end at a roadblock last week. The drink warmed my veins and relaxed my shoulders and I sat and listened and smiled and tapped my foot because I didn't know any of the words. And then one of the boys said, "Come on, Englishman, give us a song. We've been doing all the work here . . . you sing us something from your public school."

There is a moment in the chemistry of drink and the sociology of alcoholics when you reach optimum dosage. You never quite know where that is . . . it's a movable dram that peaks in the feeling that you're completely in control and that your control is balletic; you are a pilot capable of great sinuous acrobatics. Normally, this moment passes without consequence as you're standing at the urinal or queuing for the bar or caught in a circular conversation on the best way to get to Chalk Farm . . . but once in a blue moon, peak inebriation meets its moment, and this was one of those times. I pushed my chair back. Wendy grabbed my thigh and gave me a look of extreme caution and fear, but I was oblivious. I was untouchable, this was my moment . . . and I stood. Outside of church and "Happy Birthday," I have never, ever, sung in public—but I

was golden. And I opened my mouth and out came a song I'd
learned in junior school, Mr. Osborne waving a ruler like a
bandmaster's baton. I suppose what made me think of it was
the rising whiskey-fueled sense of ire and all the Saxon murder
and mocking banter that was swilling around the room. I'd
had summer and Saturday jobs on Kensington Church Street
where every other week we had bomb threats. I'd once cleared
the men's shop I was an assistant in and stood on the other side
of the road waiting for the police to come and say it was a hoax
when a woman hurried up to me and asked where her husband
was. I don't know. "But you were serving him," she said. Well,
he went into the changing room. "Didn't you check," she said.
No. Do you want to go and get him, I said. "No, you go and
get him," she replied. He's your husband. "He's your customer." I found him standing in the middle of the shop in a suit
that was far too big. There's a bomb, I said. We're evacuating.
"Oh," he replied, "Do you want me to change?" And there'd
been enough real bombs in London. I heard the one that killed
Gordon Hamilton Fairley, the cancer specialist whose dog set
off a car bomb that was meant for Sir Hugh Fraser, so there
was a rising bat squeak of "Fuck you all" in my stance. I can't
pretend that what came out of my mouth was political or committed, it was just a moment of omnipotent, golden, untouchable, witty brilliance. *"Some speak of Alexander and some of
Hercules, of Hector and Lysander and such great names as
these . . . ,"* I swelled to a Sunday baritone, as the Fenian faces
watched with a stony blankness, *"but of all the world's great
heroes there is none that can compare with a tow, row, row,*

row, row, row to the British Grenadier." If you haven't heard
this before and you're an active hands-on member of an Irish
Republican paramilitary group, then the surprise, the punch
line, is right at the end. I sat down. The bated moment hung in
the tarry air. No one moved. There was a shrill silence, and
then the man opposite me, who had said little, the man I'd
been told I should forget having ever seen, reached forward
with remarkable speed and a big practiced hand, grasped the
back of my neck and pulled my head across the table until his
face was an inch from mine and I was staring into his pale,
unreadable eyes. "You," he said quietly, but loud enough for
his voice to shiver the furniture, "you are either the bravest or
the stupidest man in all Ireland tonight." There was a beat. He
let go of my neck, rocked back in his seat and breathed out a
great guffawing laugh. The room erupted in Hibernian hilarity. My head was slapped, the pints lined up. I was so full of
retrospective adrenaline that I drank the lot of them under the
table. And as we walked home through the silent miserable
Derry streets, one of the brothers said, "You know, they were
the worst regiment we ever had here, the Grenadier Guards,
bastards . . . Kicking in doors, wrecking houses, beating the
shit out of kids . . . really vicious fucks."

The song I sang, "The British Grenadiers," was originally
Dutch, "Mars van de Jonge Prins van Friesland," brought over
to England by William, who was married to the Stuart Mary
and became our royal Bill who beat James II at the Battle of
the Boyne, just up the road from where we were, so this may

well have been the first place anyone heard that song. I was, inadvertently, bringing it home.

That would be a good rock-bottom story, an illustration of the willful out-of-controlness of drink, the edge it pushes you over. So let's leave it there and cut to the bit where I shake hands with the doctor and am hugged by other hopeful patients as I leave Clouds House rehabilitation clinic for the variously addicted and walk into a new, sober life. But it wasn't like that. I continued to drink for years after that, and the real rock bottom is when all the stories and the tales are past but their consequences litter your life, and inside, you're like . . . shell-shocked. It was just me alone in a room with the curtains pulled and the telly on, twisted and desperate with guilt and frustration. The end isn't dramatic or an exclamatory narrative, it's just when nothing works and nothing helps and there are no more angles and no more panaceas. There's nothing left to say and no one left who's listening.

But no one ever asks what the best moment of your addiction was. No one has ever said, "What was the finest drink you ever had?" But there must have been one . . . a high point. An optimum inebriation, a time when it was all golden, when the drink and the pleasure made sense and were brilliant. There was that moment. It lasted for six months. When I look back, it was everything I wanted my affair with addiction to be. In 1980, New York. I'm twenty-six, I'm in love with Amelia and in love with being in love in this city. I've been doing odd jobs, painting and decorating, being a janitor in a school up in

Harlem and in the evening I'd drink in the Dublin House—the Irish again—on the Upper West Side. A bar that had once been a speakeasy. It was everything I wanted from a pub: dark, old photos, red leather, cigarette smoke, purposeful, utilitarian, fit for its calling—a room to drink in. A long room, filled with generations of solitary thoughts. There was an old jukebox and I'd sit at one end of the bar and drink glasses of dark Beck's with Wild Turkey chasers and smoke Lucky Strikes, a combination that has never been bettered in all drunkenness. I'd read *The New York Times* and the *Post* and *The New York Review of Books*. The barman, a third-generation Irish New Yorker who still nursed a discernible Dublin Northside brogue, was friendly but taciturn. I'd wait for Amelia to finish work as a waitress at Gleeson's on the Park. She'd come in at about twelve and we'd go downtown to CBGB or the Mudd Club. I was sitting at the bar at the Dublin House when I heard John Lennon had been shot round the corner at the Dakota, and they played "Auld Lang Syne" on the jukebox all night, and the barman fed me whiskey on the house by way of apology and sympathy for a fellow deceased Brit. That was probably the best—just there, that time. And John Lennon dead.

When you stop drinking and taking drugs, people say: "Well done." "Congratulations." "What inner strength." "What grit." "What willpower." Well, the truth is exactly the opposite. All the stubborn willpower, all the straining, all the fight, goes into trying to keep going, to keep using. Stopping is surrender, putting up your hands. Living sober is nothing like as heroically gritty as trying to live stoned and drunk. So this is what really happened. I went to a doctor to pick up Melanie's daughter. Melanie was the woman who had taken me in, and whom I loved. Her daughter, Fleur, needed an injection, she was going on holiday. I avoided doctors, I didn't like them . . . I didn't want to hear what they had to say. The little girl bounced out of the consulting room, and the doctor, Guy, followed, he was about my age. I stood up to go. "Are you Adrian?" he said. "Do you want to just step into the office for a moment?" No, I've got to take Fleur home. "It's all right, she'll be fine here, it'll only take a couple of minutes." There's nothing the matter with me. "Well, Melanie is worried about you and asked me to see you." So I went into Guy's office and sat down . . . and he said it was the drinking, and I said, I thought as much, but it was fine. She was overreacting. You know women, always worrying. And he said could I answer some questions as honestly as possible. I said as long as I don't have to write the answers. And he started the standard twenty questions that are used to ascertain alcohol abuse.

On any other day I'd have lied. Any drunk worth his drink would have lied, but for some reason I told the truth. I think the fact that he was quite like me and noticeably nonjudgmental, almost unconcerned, tipped it. I appreciated the insouciance. He came to the end and said, "Well, if you answer yes to three of the questions, we consider you have a problem with alcohol. You have only answered no to two—'Have you ever lost any time off work through drink?' and 'Did you drink whilst pregnant?' I'm pretty confident in saying that you're an alcoholic." He wasn't the first person to mention it. I paused and said, Okay, what can you give me for it? "It doesn't work like that," he said. I had, by some ridiculous good fortune, stumbled upon one of the very few doctors in Britain who didn't treat alcoholism as Valium deficiency. "You should go into treatment," said Guy. "It's a new idea that's come from America. You go away to a house in the country and stay for as long as it takes, but it'll be a minimum of three weeks, and you come out with the best chance of leading a sober and clean life. The answer, I'm afraid, is abstinence. There is no controlled drinking or casual drug-taking, no exeat for Christmas or birthdays or very, very good claret." He pointed out that I would have already tried all that, tinkered with the dosages and volumes, set up numerous rules, made promises, tried to do deals with fate and God . . . and that doesn't work. "Do you have health insurance?" Of course I didn't have health insurance. "Well, I'm afraid this is going to be quite expensive." I said I'd go, and Guy said, "Can you go now?" Oh, no, no, no, no . . . I have things to do, business to settle . . . Of course I had nothing to do or settle. "When will you go?" he asked. Two weeks, a fortnight. He looked at his diary. "That's April first—is that a joke?"

The second fortunate thing was that I didn't walk out of the surgery and tell Melanie everything was fine, but she needed a new doctor . . . I went to see my dad, sobbed and asked him to pay for me to go to treatment . . . and he said how relieved and pleased he was, and did I want to do Freudian analysis instead? Miraculously, I said no. And two weeks later, I was on the train to East Knoyle in Wiltshire. My dad came with me, Melanie took us to the station and gave him a wicker basket with a gingham cloth. Inside were pork pies, a fruitcake and two bottles of vintage champagne—Dad and I drank the champagne. He had a glass, I had a bottle and a half. But I think he ate most of the pork pie. I don't know if I ever thanked my dad for taking me. At the time, obviously, I was drunk and frightened and desperate, wearing a suit with a bow tie. I remember the journey as being pleasant, like traveling through an Eric Ravilious illustration, pale, rhythmic, nostalgic. I was thirty. I didn't need him to hold my hand, but he did, because he was my dad. And now I wish I'd told him it meant a great deal to me. At the sanatorium they breathalyzed me and the nurse said she hoped I hadn't driven there. Daddy hugged me, wished me well and took the train back to London.

Two of my father's great heroes were Byron and Turner, both classical and romantic, each compellingly modern in his moment, understanding and embodying a movement, a change in the national culture. Also both were men who stepped outside their class and the assumptions of their birth. Byron is remembered as much for his life as for his poetry now, less in tune with our age than the "bed-wetter" Keats or the terminally wetter Shelley. He passed on to me the love of Turner. I've written two features on him—one strange one with David Hockney, where he insisted that Turner's great influence was plainly Rembrandt's etchings, and another about Turner's sketchbooks. He was an inveterate, almost obsessive scribbler, always had a small sketchbook to hand, drew constantly. The books are all owned by the nation, are part of the Turner

Bequest and kept at the Tate. I spent a day going through them. Like all sketchbooks, they are intimate. They are also transcendent, unguarded, never meant for public examination; they're like diaries. You can see he would often draw without looking at the paper, the pencil stub moving with a Zen-like tentative assurance; the drawings are haiku. Others are incredibly worked, topographical studies started *en plein air* and worked up in a studio. Turner's early fortune came from engravings made from travel watercolors: Swiss views and French rivers. He had a very close relationship with his father, a Covent Garden barber. His mother went mad and was consigned to an asylum. Perhaps it was the sadness of that that led Turner and his father to rely on each other. His dad paid for art lessons and then gave up the barber's shop to run his studio, which became the first commercial gallery in Britain. While I was at the Tate and looking at the pictures in the Turner wing, which I hadn't done since I was a student, I came across a painting I'd never seen before. That's not unusual: the Turner Bequest is enormous, probably the single most generous gift ever made to the nation, from a cockney boy who was regularly mocked and patronized for being common and uncouth. The pictures are circulated—some stay in storage for years. This one was an oil called *Death on a Pale Horse*, and it is unlike anything Turner ever painted before or after, not in technique but in subject. It is an image taken from the Book of Revelation, the last Rider of the Apocalypse—Death. But this is not death triumphant, this isn't the final arbiter of existence, the grim joker, the dancing master of death. Here the Reaper is himself expiring. Thrown over a horse, a collection of bones with a diadem or helmet, rotting and sick, perhaps unable to offer the final peace of death to himself. Death is exhausted and sickened by its relentless calling, its hand, great and bony, grasps for something, gestures toward the light, the horse is rearing, its gray head thrown back in anguish. It was probably taken from one of the Elgin Marbles—another reference to dead empires and the vanity of nations that is a recurring theme for the iconoclastic republican Turner. It is an amazing and distressing painting—the corrupt parcel of bones, the animal terror of the horse, the beautifully looted ruined colors of tilthy umbers and that yellow that is his hue and dye. Lawrence Gowing was the first to suggest that this unusual painting is Turner's reaction to the death of his father. He rarely lets his personal life intervene in his job as an artist, but perhaps this is singular because it is entirely private, never made to be sold or to impress the academicians or Ruskin. The golden acid lemon in the painting is still called Turner's Yellow and is the pale light of his sunsets and sunrises that so often masquerade as each other. It is actually named for another Turner—James, an English colorman, who invented a new yellow from lead oxy-fluoride and salt. Artists' palettes in the eighteenth century were short of yellows and greens, but there was also a lot of inquisitive chemistry, particularly in Germany, and Turner, J. M. W., was the beneficiary and its best advertisement for the newly realized cobalts, zinc, chrome and cadmium. You can see in the earlier Turner's snobby contemporary Reynolds the limitations and failures of the previous century's fugitive colors—in Turner there is the fantastic saturated promise that would make Impressionism and Expressionism vital. James Turner sued another colorman for transgressing his patent on the yellow and made patent history, so he called the color Patent Yellow. It was named after him on his death. When he died, he left all the paraphernalia and the patented colors to his wife on the understanding that his children would never benefit from them.

As I was going through the notebooks in the back room at the Tate, the curator asked if I'd like to see Turner's death mask. The museum had a cast of it. He produced a cardboard box and pulled out a lot of tissue paper, and then, like a magician producing a coup, he gingerly and slowly pulled out a face. I watched as through the dark of the box, the crushed and caressed paper, floated this pale visage, sans teeth, sunken-cheeked, eyes closed. It emerged into the sunlight, and with a powerful stab, a bright yellow flash, I recognized him. It was my dad. Absolutely as I remembered him. The last time I ever saw him . . . it was the image of my father on his deathbed.

I HAVE A RECURRING DAYDREAM I will wake up and find an angel at the end of my bed. He'll be played by Marius Goring, reprising his role from *A Matter of Life and Death*. Sometimes it's Henry Travers, the English character actor who gave us Clarence Odbody, the apprentice angel in *It's a Wonderful Life*. But Goring's better in the part. He holds a ledger and says, "I'm terribly sorry to wake you, don't be concerned, it's just there's been a bit of a cock-up, not your fault. It's bookkeeping. Or the computer. Anyway, something has got glitched in the system and it appears that you've been given someone else's life. Obviously, it's our fault and we're not going to charge you for it. You can have it gratis. But I'm afraid we're going to have to take the rest back. There's a poor man down the road who's been hanging around waiting for it for years. So, we'll just pack it up and get out of your way. You won't feel anything. Go back to sleep, and when you wake, well, you'll be back where you were. Snug in your own life. So enjoy, and we'll see you"— he glances at the ledger—"ah, we'll see you quite soon."

There is, with many addicts, the odd feeling that the life they've spent using was the real one, that their sober, clean life is somehow a miasma, a mirage, a cheat, a con, or just a stroke of mocking luck. It takes a long time to realize that this is also who you are. There is a fold in my life—a before and an after. And April 1 is the last date before the page is turned. The day of my last drink. Champagne with my dad on the train. It's a neat and memorable send-off, but not typical. Lots of people have obvious before-and-after moments in their lives, but for us, for me, it isn't just a milestone, it's a born-again new-person makeover. It's witness protection. I had to stop being the person I'd been and start living as someone else. To begin with, I was defined by what I wasn't anymore. I wasn't a person who drank, I was a person who didn't drink, I was a person who didn't take drugs. But then I realized you can't pick and choose what you change—everything is tainted, conspired, corrupted. Everything was a continuation of a story, a memory, anything could be a trigger, a pratfall, a collaborator with the person I was. The person I was, was dying of drink and drugs, and everything about him was enfeebling, enabling and complicit. I had to find someone else to be, to live in. I couldn't just keep the fun bits and lose the annoying stuff, because I couldn't trust myself to make those choices.

Collecting the components of a whole new person on the move as you live them is messy. I felt like a scarecrow. What do I wear? What sort of hair do I have? Have I got a beard? What pizza toppings do I like? What do I listen to? What are my favorite films? And first, most profoundly . . . who are my friends? I discovered I had surprisingly few. A couple told me they didn't want to know me if I was no longer pubbable, but then most of the folk I'd hung around with were. I drank with them, and principally that was what we had in common—or at least facilitated what we had in common. So within a few months they faded away; but I had Melanie and a community of fellow drunks and addicts trying to stay sober. The collective nature of their fellowship is something I'd never had before. We obviously had a lot in common.

I went to my first AA meeting the day after I came back to London. It was in St. Mary Abbot's Hospital. I found the room and, with a flighty suspicion and considerable fear that if I couldn't make this work, I really was on my own, I sat on the school chair at the back of the room, where half a dozen of the most miserable-looking blokes were hunched and silent. I was early. We all sat in a brown stupor for ten minutes while I thought, Is this it for the rest of my life? Is this the end I have to go to? I heard laughing and chatting in the corridor outside. I couldn't stand the depressive stillness anymore, so I shuffled out of the door, and there was a gaggle of animated people, a teapot and a plate of biscuits. And an AA meeting. I'd been sitting in the mental hospital day-care room.

The second A in AA and NA is for Anonymous. When I first walked into the room, I was told that the anonymous bit was for the protection of newcomers who felt guilty and embarrassed and shy, so we just used first names. And then the anonymity protects everybody else. We don't talk about what's said or who's who in meetings. And then I was told, finally, the anonymous bit is to protect the public from me, because I can become a really terrible proselytizing born-again bore about sobriety. So the first rule of sober club is, I don't talk about sober club.

And then I had to find something to do.

I'd already decided that I wasn't an artist—so who would this sewing-basket hastily stitched-together person be? In the past I'd signed on to for seven years, I'd been a waiter, a cook, a gardener, various sorts of shop assistant, a nanny, a painter and decorator, a warehouseman, an occasional male model. I once lectured on British film to a college class of undergraduates in Kentucky. I was film director Michael Winner's gardener for a summer. I never actually saw Michael, but I was warned that he was very keen on the roses being efficiently deadheaded.

I failed into journalism. If I'd been a better barman or painter, a better shop assistant or warehouseman or gardener, I'd have stayed doing that. Journalism is full of people who fell short at other things . . . the City, politics, secret service. Those who can't do, teach, and those who can't teach, teach PE, but those who can't even teach PE, report, and those who can't report, write columns.

At *Tatler*, I had an editor who did more to make me into a features writer than anyone else. Jo Drinkwater was an unlikely editor. She was jolly and a typical public school Sloane Ranger, who adored the royal family, knew how to address a divorced duchess, held sobbing views on the sanctity of the English countryside and the essential godly goodness of country-house weekends and Fulham dinner parties. And Earls. And cavalry regiments. She was also a naturally dexterous editor with perfect pitch for the rhythm of a sentence, and the most attractive quality of the inherited middle class: a second-nature understanding of her own ridiculousness, with a bottomless well of self-deprecation and a filthy erotic passion for tradesmen. Jo and I got on. We couldn't have been more different from or more sympathetic to each other. She took endless care and time with my cliché-ridden copy. She had public school grammar and would never have said "fewer" when she meant "less," in fact she'd never have said fewer or less . . . it would have been "enough." It was Jo who one day was going through a column, putting in paragraph breaks and reprimanding all the sentences starting with "but," who said quietly, "You know, you are a common little arriviste . . ." Yes, that goes without saying. "But what you also are is funny." Really? Weird or tee-hee? "Tee-hee . . . though you could be ha-ha. You might even manage guffaw-guffaw, but not on *Tatler*, it wouldn't be seemly. But you are a funny writer." I'm not, I'm a serious writer . . . I'm very serious about writing . . . with quite a lot of repressed rage. "No, that's not rage. You're just insecure . . . and you want to be taken seriously. And that's not the same thing. The truth is, there are lots and lots of very serious men who know far more and are far cleverer than you and they write very serious, but very, very few of them can write funny. Most of them couldn't even fall over funny. But you could, if you wanted to. Write I mean—not fall over. And if you think you want to make a living out of journalism, then make 'em laugh." But I hate funny people. They make me angry ("No . . . insecure"). I can't bear men who tell jokes. I don't think jokes are at all funny. I despise stand-up comics—they're like lap dancers, but without the honesty or the assets. They just stand in front of drunk men saying, "I can make you laugh. I can make you laugh again." They don't even have the decency to take their clothes off. "You see, that's almost funny . . . that's an amusing observation." Well, I'd never made what you'd call a living out of anything. So that sounded plausible.

I sat down at the desk with Jo and tried to be funny. We did it together. Humor in writing is mostly a series of tricks—familiar setups, misdirection, unexpected juxtaposition and rhythm. What I really learned at Jo's desk was the heartbeat pentameter of first-person writing. It's all in the pulse. And then I read a lot of funny writers—Mark Twain; Flann O'Brien ("Descartes spent far too much time in bed subject to the persistent hallucination that he was thinking"); Evelyn Waugh; A. G. Macdonell, a journalist who had a beastly shell-shocked Great War and died too young, but also wrote *England, Their England*, a book of perfect maudlin humor with the very best description of a cricket match. And of course P. G. Wodehouse. I mostly read humorous writing with a tooth-sucking detachment: it doesn't actually make me laugh. I like to see a piece of literary business done well. But only with Wodehouse is it impossible to tell how he does it. The trick of funny writing is that there is no trick, the timing is in the moving lips of the reader. There are no wings, no offstage, no trapdoors, no sound effects, no gurning at the audience to make the mood . . . except with Wodehouse. I can't see his jokes coming, and when they do, I can't tell where they've come from or how he did it. It's all there in black-and-white on a page—the story and characters are remedial, repetitive, tiresome, idiotic—but that just makes the skill more extractingly plosive, the laughter more extraordinary. And, as Jo added, "anger is best turned into wit. . . . It's far more galling for the subject to be laughed at than ranted at . . . and anyway, anger is so tiresomely middle-class." Really. "Oh yes, the upper classes are furious, never angry." I'll remember that.

Every month there would be a space for what was called the "two-page funny." A thousand words of nebulous snobbery or winsome social observation: usually a list of ten things not to say in a best man's speech; the five people your father doesn't want you to bring home for the weekend; upper-class, middle-class and lower-class excuses for everyday embarrassments; a foreigner's guide to euphemisms. And that was how I learned to be amusing in a series of sleights of syntax, syncopations of direction and long detours for a double entendre that means only one thing. Most important are alacrity and deftness with puns. Humor, in English, is not difficult. Not least because the readers of English are such pushovers for a laugh. They want it so badly, like sugar junkies outside a sweet shop. They'll forgive all sorts of grammatical and contextual transgressions if they

lead to an expected pun . . . and they also like an innuendo—
oooh, don't we all! Take the limerick. Only the English could so
utterly yearn for a giggle that they'll laugh at limericks. The
first ones written by Edward Lear are the most humorless
things ever said in jest. Laughing at "There was an old man
with an eyebrow, that was indisputably highbrow" is proof
that you will probably laugh at absolutely anything, that you
have such hair-trigger humor that you will find hilarity in the
barest litany. It is the distinguishing truth of the English that
they'll happily truffle for laughs in places where other cultures
can't even find sense. Making the English laugh is like tick-
ling children: they start squealing at the anticipation and will
squirm and chortle until you get bored. There was a craze for
limericks at the turn of the twentieth century. Newspapers ran
limerick competitions with cash prizes that were large enough
for some people to have become semiprofessional limericists.
There were self-doctored professors who would sell particularly good competition-winning rhymes. (The most expensive
and successful destination for a limerick, by the way, is Nan-
tucket . . . I'll give you that for nothing.) Almost every Edwardian poet of any distinction had a go at limericks. It was said
that they were a necessary and collectively licensed sexual
delinquency. There were supposedly three sorts of limericks—
those to be repeated when women were present—"There was a
young man from Darjeeling, who got on a bus bound for Eal-
ing, It said on the door, don't spit on the floor, so he got up and
spat on the ceiling"—those for when clergymen were present—
"A pansy who lived in Khartoum, took a lesbian up to his room,

They argued all night, about who had the right, to do what, and with what, and to whom"—and then those to be repeated when there were no clergy or ladies in earshot—"There was a young lady from Arden, who was sucking a cock in the garden, He said to her, 'Flo, pray where does it go?' To which she replied [you need to swallow theatrically here, or better, gulp from a glass] . . . 'Pardon?'"

I'm aware that this isn't a funny book, which I readily admit is a disappointment to both of us. It's about me, and I'm not really funny . . . or not very funny. I don't tickle myself . . . I'm not upper-class enough to make a joke where there is none, or working-class enough to find humor in hardship. I'm middle-class and I look up at him and think he's absurd, and I look down on him and think he's pathetic. I have no innate sense of humor. Which I find a relief. I put on humor, like working overalls or clown's trousers. It is an outer show, there is no inner conviction.

If you write in English for the British, then you have to know there is sympathy and pride in humor. It is a type of writing that I think uniquely is read as a collaboration. If people laugh, they feel understandably that they've actually contributed to the joke—indeed, it wouldn't have been a joke without the laughter. A joke that doesn't make you laugh, of course, is wit. And you grow to appreciate wit when laughing out loud gives you coughing fits and makes your back hurt. The best thing about *Tatler*—apart from Jo—was that it was a forgiving and generous place to learn how to write. It was known as a sunset-and-sunrise publication, where people came to end their careers or to start them. So there were a lot of young, funny, keen people in the office and some much older, more experienced, cynical and much funnier people to keep them in line. There was Peter Townend, a society arbiter who had been responsible for the list at the door of the Royal Enclosure at Ascot, the ultimate arbiter on who was or wasn't a deb or a deb's delight. And if you don't know what any of that means, I can't pretend it matters. He was a prickly, unattractive and spitefully gay man who was most like some malevolent but arcanely wise character from *The Lord of the Rings*, and naturally we all adored him. If you had an awkward or outré social, liturgical or hereditary problem, it was him you asked. He was like Edwardian Google. "What's the courtesy title for the second son of the Duke of Stevenage?" He'd roll his eyes and huff, as if you'd asked what color grass was, and reply, "Hitchin, of course. But it's in abeyance."

I once went to him with an inquiry about what sort of raincoat a gentleman wore in the City. He raised an eyebrow and flared his nostrils: "None. No gentleman would be seen in anything as vulgar as a mackintosh." He pronounced it as two words. "A gentleman might have a covert coat in the country." (A covert coat is named after a bit of wood; it has three seams at the bottom so that when it gets frayed after a lot of hunting, you can cut it and it won't unravel. Not many people know that.) "In town, if it's raining," he continued, "a gentleman wears a taxicab and the doorman carries an umbrella." The gossip was that Peter had fallen hopelessly in love with one of our subeditors—a very handsome public school boy.

Looks were always the first requirement for employment at *Tatler* . . . that and access to a trust fund. Victoria Mather, the travel editor, recently told me she remembered my arrival. She had lunch with the editor who told her that she must give this new writer, Adrian, as much work as she could because "he was very, very poor."

Working for *Tatler* in the '90s was like being a stationmaster on a model railway. If you lay flat on the floor and closed one eye, the world we created almost looked real. It was immensely good, harmless and, most important, pointless fun. Someone would shout across the office, "Is it acceptable to wear cuff links with a precious stone at lunch?" Howls of derision. "How long do you have to wait before banging your sister's ex-boyfriend . . . if he's got a title and a proper pheasant shoot?" I hadn't met quite so much posh totty (their description) in one place before, and I was surprised and bemused by their fathomless interest in sex. Not romantic coupling, but graphic, explicit, mechanistic farmyard covering. "Christ, have you shagged Mungo?" "Mungo TSP?" "No, er, Mungo von K." "Oh no. Snogged at the Feathers yonks ago. Sarah has." "Sarah kipper knickers?" "No, Sarah inverted nipple." Shouts . . . "Sarah, did you shag Mungo von?" "Yes, last year at Bath. Why?" "I'm going to the Heythrop Ball with him." "Oh, are you staying with Tinks and the colonel?" "No, his uncle." "It's just . . . What did you do about his todger?" "Oh, I know, it's handle with care. Fucking enorm. I thought I'd have to dislocate my jaw like a python. It's vast, like fucking a minaret." "Oh God, I wouldn't let him in downstairs—I thought I'd have to ride sidesaddle for the rest of my life. Agony. Soapy tit-wank, darling . . . the answer to unfeasibly ginormous wangers." "Well, that's fine for you, you've got melons . . . I've got oranges." "Give him a hand job . . . perfectly happy. He's grateful to anyone who'll look twice at it . . . not just huge, but hideous. It's like inheriting a really massive brick Gothic house in Nottinghamshire. You know you ought to be pleased, but all you can think of is the maintenance . . . going up and down, up and down, from attic to cellar . . . and all that polishing. Tell you what, why don't we do a list . . . Top nobs with knobs on." "No, better . . . Toffs with yobs' knobs."

That's pretty much verbatim. Even though it was over a quarter century ago, you don't forget dialogue of that quality. An awful lot of what we did was lists and rules. An absurd amount of amusement in copy was gleaned from people saying "mirror" instead of "glass," and not knowing the difference between a stock, a cravat, an Ascot and a gentleman's square. Like capricious social health and safety officers, the girls at *Tatler* could make up rules for absolutely anything. Lists are ubiquitous and annoying, like takeaway coffee menus. Ours were handcrafted and made with pride and hilarity.

The light reverential mockery of class was the compost of *Tatler.* I expect we'd have said it was the rich loam on which the nation was built. We understood that the defining character of the English was the rift between those who HKLP and those who didn't HKLP: Hold Knife Like Pen. If you needed that spelled out, as once I did, then mark yourself down a peg, and the next time you say it and have to explain it to someone else, you can step up a rung. The point about snobbery and its thousands of raised-eyebrow, nose-tapping rules is that you can't simply progress up the scale by the very nature of the thing—others must descend. We mocked and joked and made puns about it because to treat it seriously, even for the briefest moment, would be surreal. Snobbery is an untenably vile web of power patronage, wholly unearned, undeserved and unfair privilege. It bears no relation to any of the human attributes, learned or inherited, that add to the good of the nation. And the sort of nostalgic hysterical snobbery we peddled has now virtually gone. Snobbery itself, of course, hasn't gone. It is still essentially the mark of insecurity. Snobbery is like peeing in your own pants. For a moment you feel relieved and a warmth . . . but everyone can see you've done it, and you're left feeling embarrassed and uncomfortable. It isn't the snobbery that's particularly English, it is the uncertainty, the lack of self-confidence, of which snobbery is such an antisocial symptom. You can always sell periodicals and newspapers to the British by reassuring them that they are the right people in the right place, but you will sell twice as many by making them think they should be someone else somewhere else.

As I was writing for *Tatler*, the rest of the press was enjoying a bit of a purple patch. Papers would boastfully halloo their monthly readership figures. The cost of newsprint and printing was falling, advertising of all sorts of soft, expensive and chic consumer stuff was rising, there was no Internet to speak of—downloading a picture on a computer took an hour and sounded like it was making a smoothie. So weekend papers added ever more supplements and magazines because the advertisers wanted glossy paper and didn't want to hawk their wares next door to murders and stock market news. Editors were in the market for some popular culture features, but not many traditional journalists could or wanted to write that kind of stuff. It had always been considered women's-page issues, so they started press-ganging from magazines to get writers to go to consumer journalism. Andrew Neil, the *Sunday Times* editor, took Christa D'Souza, a very sharp, funny and smart interviewer from *Tatler*, and she in turn said he should read me. So I started to write small pieces for the newly made Style and Travel sections. Generally, Style was social comment on something that had happened in the week. We went to press on Thursdays and didn't really know what the story would be until Tuesday. So you had to write fast to a brief. Speed and dependability are the essence of newspaper writing. I loved it. I was uncluttered with the rules and best practices of reporting. It was fun. We'd make up the section as we went along, bringing the bravado of magazines to the immediacy and directness of papers. I once had to spend a day walking round London dressed as Mr. Darcy. I was sent to learn ballroom dancing with a lot of pensioners. I was put on a plane to Prague to discover if it was going to be the new Paris for American novelists. (It wasn't. But I still had to find a story and my photographer never turned up, so I had to find a snapper as well.) We had a tough but capricious editor, Alison McDonald, who again took endless trouble with my copy. The section varied in quality and was often a mess, but it was always vital and irreverent and usually funny, and there was nothing else like it.

So after a bit, the *Daily Telegraph* offered me a job and I called Alison and told her. I didn't really have any desire or intention of going to the *Telegraph*, it was just a bit of gossip. Five minutes later, she called me back and asked what I was doing. I was cooking supper. Boiled brisket. "I'm coming over," she said. And was soon in the kitchen with a glass of wine and a cigarette and said, "Andrew wants to offer you a contract, and you're not under any circumstances to talk to the *Telegraph*." Oh, okay. And then she added, "That's a good thing, Adrian."

Tony Rennell, the news editor, took me to lunch at the Savoy Grill and asked me what I wanted from journalism. I had no idea. I said the first glib thing that came into my head . . . that I wanted to go and interview places, as if they were people. It was a phrase that followed me around and became prophetic. Quite a lot of my career has been interviewing places. But in my head I think of them as, if not people, then cognizant entities with personalities . . . a sort of civic-morphism. "You're a good writer," said Tony. "But there are lots of good writers. The thing with you is that you're a lucky writer, and we can't teach that." And then I had to go and discuss my contract with Tony Bambridge, the managing editor. The two Tonys were the axis around which the newspaper ran; in the newsroom, they were collectively known as the Tonton Macoute. I went into Tony Bambridge's office. He was sitting behind the desk in shirtsleeves. Shirtsleeves were the office uniform, with a loosened tie, and quite often suspenders. The editor wore suspenders. And the newsroom was then as male and hierarchical as a prep school. He laced his fingers behind his head and said, "Okay. Adrian, you've got us. We want you. Make the most of it." I liked Tony Bambridge, he was a journalist from Central Casting, a cockney communist who looked as neat and smart as a gangster. He was tough and sentimental, and he was always very good to me. He told me what they wanted me to write and said, "We'll pay you this." And he slid a piece of paper across the desk. I turned it over. It was a frankly frightening amount of money. Indeed, it was more money than I'd ever earned . . . all put together, everything. Journalists didn't have agents then, and the union had been banished, so I had no idea about what anyone else made. In fact, it was in all our contracts that we couldn't tell anyone what we made. I just knew it was a great deal more than *Tatler* paid, and I also knew that you weren't supposed to accept the first offer, so I slid the paper back and said, I don't think that's really enough. Tony gave me a look of mocking surprise. "Not enough? And how much do you want to earn?" I had no idea. What were you supposed to ask for—double? Ten percent? Another couple of quid? I said I wanted to earn more than my father. "Oh my lord," he said. "Sons. The bleeding ingratitude of sons. I've got two. Okay, how much does your dad make?" I had no idea. So I added five grand to the figure he'd offered. He snorted and wrote another number on the paper. Slid it back. It was the figure I'd asked, plus two thousand pounds more. I said it was a deal. "Are you going to tell your dad you said that?" Pass me the phone, I said. It rang twice, my father answered. Dad, it's Adrian. I'm sitting in the managing editor's office at *The Sunday Times* and they just offered me a contract. "Oh, good," he said softly, in the amused, disbelieving tone he used for optimistic news. "I'm pleased." I looked over at Tony . . . And they're paying me more than you make. Without missing a beat, Dad grew serious and said, "Oh yes, I should think so . . . I was earning a lot more than my father when I was your age."

The funny thing is, he'd always said I should be a journalist. He'd been a journalist on *The Observer* and *The Scotsman*. A subeditor. When I was a teenager and we really weren't getting along, he'd say, "You'd be a very good journalist." And I'd shimmy with rage . . . How can I be a fucking journalist when I can't fucking write? Writing being a fucking prerequisite for journalism. "And you'd be a good teacher," he'd add. "You should teach." I haven't got a single exam, I said. I left school at seventeen, and I still can't write. Which is also a prerequisite for teaching. Occasionally now I'm asked to go and teach a class with postgraduate journalism students, and every time I walk into the room, I think of my dad, and that soft, disbelieving tone of voice saying, "I told you so." When I first wrote, it was like walking into a room that I was completely familiar with but that I'd never been in before. There was a profound sense of coming home as I started to write . . . always in the first person. I immediately realized that this was what I'd been trying to do in studios with pencils and paint—I'd been using the wrong language. Recently I read something that I wrote twenty-eight years ago, and what struck me was the cockiness, the unbelievable confidence of it. There is no doubt, no throat clearing, no hesitation . . . the style and tone are already there. It is the same style and tone that I'm writing this in now. I didn't have to discover a voice, just a medium, and the implication is that I should have been writing all along, that I wasted school and college doing the wrong thing. But actually one of the things that helped me as a writer was that I came to it late. I didn't really start till I was nearly forty. Everyone I was competing with was ten years younger than me. They had emerged from university, where they'd read English or Classics or PPE (philosophy, politics and economics) and they were fluent and brittle and glib and fluffy, blinking in the sunlight. Most of them knew everything and had experienced virtually nothing. I, on the other hand, knew nothing about writing. I still don't understand the first thing about grammar, I wasn't steeped in literature or Latin or languages, but I had done lots and lots of menial things, of disreputable, humiliating, repetitive, pointless things. I spent a lot of time with people who did them all their lives. Months and years in pubs, on benches, waiting at bus stops and in squats . . . I'd spent all the time not writing, but talking and listening and being acutely aware that I was wasting my time—first in trickles and then in torrents. I was unaware that actually I wasn't wasting time, I was banking it, and I discovered that in writing and in cooking and gardening and fucking and whist, experience always trumps cleverness. There is no substitute for having been there and got it under your fingernails. I had just done, been and seen a lot more than most other young style writers and opinionators, and that not writing had made me talk, and that talking had given me a long vocabulary and a more acute ear for rhythm. Coming as I did from a family who talked all the time, who learned and performed lines, I had an innate fascination with and reverence for words, as if I'd always known that they were really mine. And art wasn't a waste of time. It made me look, as opposed to merely see—nothing makes you examine space like having to draw it.

Those thousands of hours spent learning the wrong thing left me with an analytical eye combined with a natural skepticism for rooms and groups and relationships. I don't know a drunk or a junkie who can't decipher the relationships and the power and the insecurity and the vanity in a room. We are alert to the small changes in alliance and humor, we're so used to being on the outside, of being supplicants and apologists. Mendacious, duplicitous, wounded, we examine minutely and see everything. When Tony Rennell said I was a lucky journalist he was half right . . . I had had a conspicuously luck-lacking life, but it made me an observant journalist. A skill honed through not being able to write, being not very good at everything I'd set my hand to, except substance abuse and recognizing a vanishing point when I see one. Cyril Connolly wrote that literature is the art of writing something that will be read twice; journalism, what will be grasped at once. I like that. I didn't have to think twice, I knew as soon as I wrote my first story that I wanted to be a journalist, and everything I'm good at, have ever wanted, desired or cared about, needs to be grasped at once. I found the thing I was meant to do. Meant to be. I'd come home. Connolly, incidentally, was also a critic at *The Sunday Times*.

I liked working for Andrew Neil. He cared about something either a lot or not at all. He was that rare thing, a working-class Paisley conservative. He would say, "I'm a real Scot. You're a reel Scot." The first major spread I did for Style, my first proper story, could have been a classic *Tatler* feature: the English in the Highlands, and the odd cocktail party that occurred at Inverness airport on Sundays when the terminal was just a hut. Here departing Sloaney families with rod and gun would meet the incoming families arriving for their weeks to bang about in the heather and there would be a braying frot of tweed and feathers. They all knew one another and would drawl with that distinctive, infuriating self-confidence that is always on broadcast, never receive; and around them hard-handed short men in baggy estate tweed suits would shoulder their dressing-up luggage. Andrew wanted that and all that. They sent a photographer up to take a picture. Did I have a kilt? the editor asked. Of course I had a kilt. We were having a midgy holiday in a little cottage with my new toddling daughter up the end of a blind glen, Strathconon. The nearest newsagent was a petrol station seven miles away. I drove my old £400 Land Rover down the glen to get milk and the papers and threw them onto the bench seat and drove back to the cottage. The magazine section slid out of the folded paper, and there was me, looking histrionically ridiculous, on the cover of Style . . . I nearly drove into the loch. Andrew asked me to be the TV critic of the new Culture section—he said he wanted what Clive James had done for *The Observer*. I said yes immediately, because I'd have said yes to anything . . . but also because I love television. I grew up in a household that made television. I am the same age as television—ITV started in 1954, the year I was born—and beyond anything else, it is the defining culture of my life. It was also one of the most undervalued corners of newspapers. Britain has an odd tradition of retrospective TV criticism, inexplicable to most other countries—why would you want to read about something that's already been and gone? Originally, papers asked theater critics to review stuff on this new box, so they wrote overnight reviews as they would for the stage, and the habit stuck. But television became a backwater for all the old, usually drunk hacks you couldn't fire because they'd been on staff too long and couldn't be trusted with anything more important; or it was given to character writers and guest novelists whose bylines were bigger than their critical talent. The roll call of truly awful TV critics included Roy Hattersley and A. N. Wilson, and, on *The Sunday Times*, Dennis Potter, who was not just lazily glib and ghastly as a writer, but sniffily sanctimonious about everything on the screen that wasn't written by him. Hattersley watched only *Coronation Street*, in a sort of knowing socialist way, and Wilson hated the medium altogether. Indeed, a lot of TV critics come to it with a broad contempt for television and the people who make and appear on it. It was always the bastard homunculus of theater, film or book, and was really memorable only when it led the audience back to its ancestors and betters, so TV reviewers would constantly review adaptations of classics by saying they hoped viewers would now go and read Austen/Brontë. The only people who were bright, intelligent and readable about the box were Clive James and Nancy Banks-Smith. But equally, television was plainly a marvelous place to write about; all human life passed through it. It was the electric Tiber. In the end, everyone you knew floated past. And the rule of criticizing anything is, first you must love it, innately, the thing itself, the idea of it, the application of it. If you don't wholeheartedly adore the medium, then why would you ever care if someone did it badly or well? So I happily did TV and was given a gratifying amount of space— normally TV columns are five hundred to eight hundred words; I had a double page and thirteen hundred words. I also wrote a weekly political column. I don't love politics, though I'm interested and committed and I enjoy covering elections, but this column made me furious every Friday. It was supposed to be funny, and sometimes it was, but I found it frustrating and frightening. Craig Brown had invented the best column on the paper—"Table Talk." A clever and quirky reimagining of the cliché-ridden ". . . and my partner had" restaurant review. He left the paper, and the column fell vacant. I asked the deputy editor, Sue Douglas, if I could have a go at it. "No," she said, I already did two columns. I'd happily give up the politics. "No, we like the politics." I sulked and nagged until I got a message that said succinctly, "Just fucking do your fucking job." So they auditioned the "Table Talk" column and gave everyone who had ever owned teeth and a functioning colon two editions to write. Each Sunday breakfast there was a grim chichi tasting menu of terrible try-hard efforts that floated past. After six months, I got another message from Sue Douglas. "I had a genius idea . . . Why don't you do the 'Table Talk' column?" One of the first reviews I did was of a Michelin star restaurant in lovely North Wales, Plas Bodegroes, where Chris Chown, whose basement Cressida and I had lived in, had given up accountancy to go and run a small hotel. Snowdonia is pretty enough if you've never seen Scotland, on the day or two it isn't raining, but the man-made bits of North Wales are grim, and I made a few flippant but fair remarks about the North Walian temperament and the nature of Mold and Flint (not as nice as they sound) and said that in general, the Welsh were loquacious dissemblers, immoral liars, stunted, bigoted, dark, ugly pugnacious little trolls. I should have added thin-skinned.

The newly opened National Assembly had a vote of censure and dispatched a policeman to arrest me. I imagined he'd be like Attila Rees, Dylan Thomas's constable from *Under Milk Wood* who piddles in his helmet. I expect he's still pedaling slowly to London. They took me to the Race Relations Board, who I think concluded that you couldn't be racist against the Welsh, and the Press Complaints Commission, who said it was satire and fair comment. I discovered that if you really want to fill your postbag with spittle-flecked viridian ire, then write something derogatory about a place. People will put up with any amount of criticism about more personal things—their professions, their hobbies, their football teams, their dress sense, their accent—but say something even mildly astringent about the village their mother was born in, and the red mist descends and out comes the green ink. That stuff about the Welsh was written over twenty years ago, but still it's the thing I'm asked about most often, and most often by Welsh people. When confronted, I always preempt the finger-wagging by asking if they're North or South Walian, and then saying I was referring to the other lot. Invariably they'll beam and say, "Oh right, well, we couldn't agree more. I think you let them off a bit lightly."

Writing about food and restaurants was lucky. The choice in journalism, as in evolution, is eternally whether to be a generalist or a specialist. My forte was that my specialism became ubiquitous. When I started, there were half a dozen readable food writers and perhaps about two dozen good restaurants. I got into it because I thought it was such a small pool it would be easier to look good. The ravenous appetite for everything to do with eating has been inexplicable, because as people consume more cookery books, they cook less. As they eat out more, so menus grow less sophisticated; the more people know about food, the less they know about eating. It is a weird contrarianism that goes to the heart of our relationship with catching, getting and sharing food. The confusion between want and need, hunger and appetite. I found that I was a good critic. The first question you should ask any critic is: How good a critic are you? And they should be able to tell you without dissembling or boasting, they should know. If they don't know, or don't want to say, then you have your answer. Criticism is above and beyond anything else being scrupulously, unswervingly, relentlessly honest . . . and you have to start on yourself. Very, very few people are cut out to be critics, or would care to be. Everyone has an opinion. Criticism isn't having an opinion, it's having a value-added opinion. Some opinions are worth more than others—mine is worth more than most. There is no upside, no benefit to being critical, it doesn't improve your enjoyment or whatever it is you're criticizing. A film doesn't miraculously become a better film because you've reviewed it, a joke isn't funnier, a song more lyrical. Ninety-nine out of a hundred art consumers will simply be thankful for the stuff that moved them and forget the stuff that didn't. Only the odd one will need to pull apart the experience, dissect the corpse of a performance, because they have some inner compulsion to understand why it worked and how it failed. But that one is a vital part of all culture. My job as a critic isn't to change restaurants for the better or improve television, it's to sell newspapers. But critics are the traffic wardens of culture—cumulatively they keep it moving.

Criticism is fascinating, complicated, eliding and contrary. It is to be constantly running your haberdasher's fingers against the lie of nap. Our natural inclination is to be kind and encouraging, to stroke the fur the way it lies at its softest. We want artists to be successful, because we understand their special role, sense their vulnerability and value the importance of their creation. The insistent motivation of the critic is not to be disinterested: they aren't searching for a legal or binding judgment, they just have to know better. Better than everyone else who is having his one singular experience—and not many can face doing that and even fewer would want to. There is, though, a deep satisfaction in being able to unpick a thing. It isn't the pleasure of making or destroying, it is almost scientific. A mathematical pleasure of understanding, discovering the pattern that is already there, already made, and palpable, but whose working is opaque, where the creator can't really describe his own process. Criticism is like being able to unbake a cake. When people fatuously ask why I don't write constructive criticism, I tell them there is no such thing. Critics do deconstructive criticism. If you want compliments, phone your mother.

The editor of *The Sunday Times Magazine*, Robin Morgan, asked me if I'd be interested in doing a feature about a famine in Sudan. Sure, I said. "I mean going to South Sudan and reporting," he said. South Sudan, where there's a civil war and the Janjaweed murderous Arab Muslim militia terrorize civilians and where there's now a famine? "Yes," said Robin, "that's the one." Paul Lowe, a photographer who'd worked in the Balkans and Chechnya, had arranged to travel with Médecins Sans Frontières; they needed someone to do the words. I'd never done anything like this. Not any proper reporting. Certainly not disasters or war. I was immediately overwhelmed by that old school feeling that I was bound to fail, and I examined in ever more graphic detail all the things that could, and therefore would, undoubtedly go wrong. I changed my mind daily. What settled it was a note I got from an editor on another section, seriously cautioning me: "Potentially you've got a good and long career on this paper, but you will be jeopardizing both your reputation and the reputation of *The Sunday Times* if you agree to go to Sudan. Sending a food critic to cover a famine was the most tasteless, embarrassing and ridiculous idea." So I called Robin and said I'd do it.

I was supposed to pick up my visa from the rebel SLA, Sudan Liberation Army, at their consulate in Nairobi—except nobody was at their consulate. I was hitching a lift into Sudan with ITN, the Independent Television Network, via Lokichogio, an extraordinary Bond-like landing strip in the desert of northern Kenya with a runway that jumbo jets can land on, surrounded by huge warehouses full of grain and rice, blankets and tents. I didn't have the visa and so I didn't take my passport. Traveling across borders without a passport isn't a great idea at the best of times. MSF said if the SLA weren't in the refugee camp, I'd probably be okay, we'd be there for only a couple of days. We flew in a little Cessna Caravan prop plane— it took hours. We landed on a strip in the bush and ran into a pothole. The ITN crew got out and said there were soldiers at the end of the runway; my MSF minder said she couldn't be associated with me because it might jeopardize their work. The Dutch pilot said that if I lay down in the back of the plane, he'd fly me back to Loki and I'd be able to hitch a lift to Nairobi in a couple of days. The thought of the long trip back to London without a story was worse than facing the guerrillas, so I got out with Paul and marched up through the bush to a little clearing that passed as an arrivals lounge, and there was a table, behind which sat a rebel general, flanked by his soldiers casually armed with pistols, Kalashnikovs, machetes and cattle whips as an unnecessary symbol of authority. They all wore shades and obsidian faces of stony hostility . . . I remember one had a baseball cap that said "Men in Black." The general watched me approach, I beamed at him. Hello, I'm Adrian Gill from *The Sunday Times* in London. I passed over my press card. I've come all this way to tell your story—we're desperately concerned to know how everything's going. He looked at me for a moment, smiled with a comical lack of front teeth, handed me back my card and said, "You're very welcome." He could spare only a few minutes, but his men would offer any assistance I needed—but I must be careful, there was a war on, you know, and there were some bad people abroad. It was a relief of enormous proportions. Possibly the greatest relief I've ever felt in my life. The ground seemed to fall away; as I walked back down the runway I was completely weightless. Suddenly I could smell and hear again: in the distance the little Caravan revved its engines for takeoff.

We got to a small MSF feeding center and sat round the campfire, eating sandwiches we'd put in our pockets in Nairobi. The news crew opened bottles of Scotch and told war stories, and around us in the dark a million starving Dinka tried to sleep. I felt chokingly ecstatic. To be in this place with this stomach-twisting, angry story: I knew beyond doubt that this was what I wanted to do for the rest of my life. Nothing else could be as completely enfolding and compelling and in the moment as this. Following the scene, the sound and the skein of a tragic story, everything I'd ever looked for in drink and drugs, and all the barmy pockets of displacement activity that came with them, was here in concentration, so intense, so clear, that there was nothing else.

I got back. The story didn't quite write itself, but the narrative of it and the images were so clear and bold that it was an arrangement rather than a construction, and Paul's pictures were an unwavering accompaniment. It worked. Another editor passed me in a corridor and without looking up said, "Turns out that a restaurant critic is exactly the person to send to a famine."

I have a bad reputation among photographers. They can be monumental Day-Glo knobs who insist on taking pictures for stories that are not going to be written and who show disdain for the one that is; who think that I'm there to write their picture captions; who want to come back to a place at five because the light will be much better then, when we're never coming back here ever again; who want to spend an hour arranging the old man and the schoolgirl in front of the temple; and more to the spiky end of the point . . . it's photographers who get you killed. Nothing alters the atmosphere like a demanding, oblivious snapper dressed in semi-military fatigues, strung about with kit bags, pointing long lenses into people's faces, shouting: ". . . ignore me. No, no . . . look down . . . Just do what you were doing." They believe their cameras are the amulets of protection. Their role model is invariably the war photographer Robert Capa, who said, "If your pictures aren't good enough, you're not close enough." They all quote that. Just after he said it, he stepped on a landmine. They are driven by competition and envy much more than writers are; a newsworthy image can make them a small fortune, but generally they're paid very little and there are dozens of wannabe Don

McCullins hitching into war zones, blithely insouciant to the risks they are taking with themselves and those who travel with them. And now that everyone has a camera in their pocket and everything's being photographed all the time, they feel the pressure. More photographs will be taken this year than in the whole history of photography—and they're all online. It's tough for photographers. Though I wish more of them knew Capa's more profound observation: "The pictures are there, all you do is take them."

Despite my reputation for being unforgiving and unhelpful to photographers, traveling with them has been the most fun and some of the most intense work I've had. I've made close friendships, sometimes just for days, sometimes for life, and the most rewarding professional times have all been shared with a monkey. Journalists call them "monkeys" because they're always climbing up things, and you really don't want to eat opposite one. Paul Lowe and I went on to do stories on drug-resistant TB and the Aral Sea, and I worked with the marvelously Eeyore-ish Peter Marlow, president of Magnum. He shot a fantastic set in Peshawar and then an equally astringent story in the Russian enclave of Kaliningrad. He brought a Rolleiflex camera that you keep on your chest as you look down into reflecting mirrors. It's slow and it shoots only a handful of frames. The film doesn't have sprockets, and he was constantly loading and unloading it. Why did you bring that ridiculous camera? I asked. "Well, when you take pictures in countries that were Communist and that had the secret police, people are very nervous of cameras pointed at them by strangers. A Rolleiflex would never be used by the KGB." It was such a thoughtful consideration, I never complained again. Peter stopped coming on jobs with me when he got fed up taking my picture. We did one story with Jeremy Clarkson where Peter ended up running up and down a gay beach in Mykonos snapping naked men. It was a low point in his Magnum career.

Jeremy and I had an even worse reputation with photographers. In Reykjavík, our monkey got into a fight with a fisherman in a bar. Jeremy and I discussed whether professional camaraderie demanded that we get involved, but decided that we were in fact in different professions and were excused fights with Vikings. The monkey was decked and thrown out. The next morning at breakfast, he appeared with a thick lip and asked if we'd picked up his camera bag. Yes, I said, here it is. "Oh thank God," he said. "And the lens bag?" What lens bag?

I did a couple of African jobs with Tom Stoddart—two kilometers down a gold mine on a newly blown face that was four feet high, where the rock was too hot to touch and had been formed when the sky was still red. He lit the portrait of me, directing the miners with their headlamps. It's a good picture. I look terrified. And the story in Uganda about an epidemic of sleeping sickness spread by migration and refugees. Tom showed me that if you're taking pictures of sick people in bed, you should never stand over them, but always get down to their level. "It's wrong to take a godlike stance over suffering," he said. "It's colonial." Tom doesn't say much, but what he does say is usually written by a Methodist sign writer outside a chapel. There was only one modern drug to treat sleeping sickness—a disease whose name belies the vileness of its contamination. It's correctly known as HAT—human African trypanosomiasis. The pharmaceutical company that made it was going to stop because people who catch sleeping sickness can rarely pay for expensive drugs, but it wasn't going to waste, they were going to rebrand it as a cosmetic depilatory for Hispanic women. It was a story of hideously impotent furious tears. I wrote it. Tom's pictures showed it. And we had the familiar default feeling of crusading journalism, which is shouting into a prevailing wind that whips the words away into the roar of traffic. But a friend, Christiane Amanpour, the CNN reporter, read the piece on an airplane and turned it into a documentary segment for American news . . . and the pharmaceutical company had a change of heart and decided they could continue manufacturing it after all. That's the power of broadcast news. But also a reminder that most stories still originate in print.

I did a couple of jobs with Harriet Logan—cataract operations and river blindness in Ghana, and the war in Iraq. She was idiotically cool when we were rocketed in a small helicopter and she filmed a race that Clarkson and I had in American Abrams tanks along the Boulevard of Martyrs in Baghdad, the street with the great crossed scimitars—you can see it on YouTube. I won. And one with the marvelously named Gigi Cohen, the most terrifying job, during a coup in Haiti. She continued to take pictures while a teenager was shot to death in a gang fight in front of us and fought a riot policeman for her camera.

I once did a job at a country fair with Don McCullin. He

made an evocative book about the English countryside when he was back from the wars. He's dry and funny and shoots only in black-and-white and never with flash. We had dinner afterward and he told a lot of hair-raising and chillingly dangerous war stories. He's a lugubrious raconteur, always being blown up and shot, left behind, threatened. He paused every so often to ask if there was garlic in this because he didn't think it agreed with him . . . and was I sure this mushroom wasn't poisonous, as if his plate were a booby-trapped paddy field in Da Nang.

Snowdon—old people and fancy bantams. You could never accuse him of snobbery: he treated them both exactly the same. I'm very fond of Tony, but he could be a bugger just for the devilment of it. Rena Effendi came to Congo and the Bekaa Valley. She was a brilliantly sympathetic photographer, particularly with traumatized and vulnerable women. She used a Hasselblad and spoke gently and encouragingly to Congolese women who had seen their families murdered and been taken as sex slaves and war-booty wives; and a gentle, haunted woman who had lived a solitary life at the edge of a village. Her husband had died in her arms, and the Lord's Resistance Army had cut off her lips with a machete. "They fell into my lap like a doughnut," she said.

The photographer I've worked with most often is Tom Craig. I've lost track of how many trips we've made, from being dug out of a blizzard in Arctic Spitsbergen to being hunted in a nighttime forest by a fossa in Madagascar, from Calcutta to Lampedusa, from Tasmania to the Towton battlefield in Yorkshire. We go easily together and have a rhythm and a routine—

his obsessive packing, my obsessive earliness. We understand closely how the other works and talk constantly about stories as they take shape, like a box made by two carpenters. Tom held an exhibition of photos from the stories we'd done together where my words really were reduced to picture captions. Our first one was to Chad and was part of a book project he was doing with MSF to accompany writers to troubled places. We were going to see more Sudanese refugees, this time from Darfur, and it was on this trip that I had the best drink I've ever swallowed. We had to make a long drive across the Sahara, it was the hottest thing I've ever experienced. The thermometer broke at 56 degrees—Celsius. We were in a truck, and after an hour I discovered that the water in my bottle was sour and Tom's bottle was empty. By the time we got to a smugglers' town that straddled the border, we were deliriously parched. We were dropped at an emergency clinic, which was a couple of hammocks in a ruined house with a generator that ran a fridge. We were greeted by a nurse of preternatural beauty—we may have just been in the sun too long, but she really was gorgeous— who said, "I'm not allowed to keep anything but medicine in the fridge, but I knew you had a long trip, so I snuck in two bottles of Fanta. Don't tell anyone." I have never swallowed anything that tasted quite so wonderful.

Over the years I've been drawn to stories about refugees, moved by their bravery, their stoicism, their sorrow, their precious ambitions and their stories. Refugee journeys are so monumental and so mundane in a world where the rest of us just get on a plane and go to sleep. What they want would count as small failures to us; the treks are more parlous and tougher, more extraordinary than any that First World adventurers and charity explorers take on. The danger and the desperate fear of the odysseys that Eritrean teenagers escaping lifelong conscription make is barely conceivable for any European. The forced movement of people around the world, the push of intolerance, starvation and murder and the pull of work, education, opportunity and safety is becoming the leitmotif at the beginning of this new century. I know it is a story that will never stop being what I want to write about. I'm not entirely sure why, of all the compelling and exotic and exciting stories in the world, this one sticks with me. But these things are never accidental. There is some hint of kindred empathy, no similarity, but there is something I identify with . . . perhaps it's to do with Nick's disappearance, perhaps it's just First World guilt? I wrote in the first Sudanese article that "it wasn't staring into the face of starvation that thuds like a blow to your heart, it is having starvation stare back at you," and that is still the truth that has been tested and remains. Tom and I covered the wreckage that washes up around the island of Lampedusa, and I wrote then that if you would come face-to-face with these people, you would never turn them away. You could not but help them. We all of us strive to be good, to be decent, to do the right thing. It is only their anonymity that allows us to support policies that turn our back on them, send them away, bury them in internment camps and embargoes. It is perfectly simple—if you were confronted with their humanity, then simultaneously you would be confronted with your own. I want to write that over and over and over again. And then I made a porn movie.

Hot House Tales was commissioned in a week and written over a weekend, and a fortnight later I was in the suburbs of Los Angeles on a set directing actors—exhibitionist sportsmen rather—on the best angle to have a threesome and how to remember their lines. "Hey, Adrian, could he fuck me in the anal here?" I don't know. Do you think your character would do that? "Yeah, I think she would. Definitely she would." Okay, well, let's try it your way. I am the only auteur in the history of old pre-Internet porn who actually used his own name on the credits. I took Nicola and a photographer whose name I forget, who was so timidly disgusted he could barely open his eyes, and turned his head away to click and then gave up altogether and sat in his motel watching the Disney Channel as a spiritual antidote. I, on the other free hand, laughed more than I have ever laughed on any story. Dangerous, weeping laughter. I had a cameraman who had a phobic fear of sperm and my male star was Ron Jeremy, a properly funny man with his clothes on, hysterically repellent with them off. The porn stars were very funny—sometimes intentionally. They were also sweet, stupid, pneumatic and very nice to each other. It's amazing how fast you can get used to having conversations with men who are lazily tugging at themselves to maintain their professional standing. The only uncircumcised member of the cast belonged to an energetic English actor whose specialty was cunnilingus. They called him the Hummingbird. Over a long frenetic career, he had actually managed to wear a hole in his foreskin—well, you just had to laugh. It was a singular story, so freighted with preconceptions, nothing was what I thought it was going to be. Things I thought would disgust and offend turned out to be hilarious and touching, stuff I thought would be fun and erotic was awkward and clumsy and sad and it put me off ever watching pornography for amusement or relief. "You know something?" the fat, hairy, gnarly-knobbed Ron said to me prophetically. "You are going to be the last generation that wanks from memory. I do it for money."

Foreign correspondents are an odd lot. They drink and fornicate as self-medication. They're twitchy and prone to be mawkish and maudlin; they're self-deprecating but rarely cynical, always parking the anger somewhere where it won't get out and lacerate someone. They also suffer from print shellshock—a sort of hacks' PTSD—paper traumatic stress disorder, an awkward itchiness in safe places, a yearning to be back in some bit of blasted world, a crawling feeling that safe and rich isn't normal. I'm not one of them, I don't suffer from it. I don't have the commitment or the thousand-yard stare. I do too many five-star hotels and five-course dinners. I'm a disaster tourist. But I do like hanging around them. Whilst they're secretive and judgmental in print, they are collaborative and helpful on the job. Being in a hacks' hotel in a disaster is contrarily brilliant; the stories throw everything into relief. There is the fraternity of inquiry and mutual concern—people share logistics and information and look out for one another (with one or two notorious and despised exceptions). It is in

those moments that you're completely aware of life and purpose. Foreign correspondent is the most unequivocally pure
form of journalism. It is going out over the horizon to catch
the news and bring it home.

I don't suffer the print trauma, but over the years I've been
aware of something else—the uncanny presence of parallel
lives. I did a story with Tom about the Forest of Dean . . . a
strange place on the edge of England. We went deep into the
wood with the Wicca people, witches, to find an ancient magic
tree. While he snapped, I walked off on my own for a spell. The
wood was silent and still. It wore its great age and the accumu-
lation of seasons with a shimmering gravitas. I had a prickling
feeling that I wasn't alone. I walked down a deer track convinced that something or someone was shadowing me in parallel. After a bit the path came to a clearing, an afternoon sunlit
meadow. I stopped in the shadows beside a humpy beech. From
the other side of the tree stepped a large, glossy dog fox. He
walked unconcerned into the sunlight, glowing like burnished
copper, and paused to look back at me from a few yards,
unafraid, with an expression that was searching and potent
and full of deep zoomorphism. Then he trotted on across the
meadow and into the shadows on the other side. And I walked
back and told the witch. She grinned and said, "Of course. I
knew you'd meet your familiar. Your companion creature. You
have a sensitivity for these things, a strong empathy." That feeling of solitary travel but of not being alone, of lives moving
beside you, just out of sight, is insistent and strong. Over the
years I've met and worked with dozens . . . hundreds of people.

We form intense connections because of what we're doing. It's very concentrated. The places and experiences are raw and exciting—often terrifying. The meetings are only for a short time, merely in passing, and they are never repeated. We exchange numbers and addresses and fraternal hugs, but we know as we wave from the departure gate that we will never meet again. These encounters are like brushing through fields of lilies: the stamens leave indelible trails of pollen, they strike me with a sweetness of something, an encounter, shared experiences. These memories and characters from the back of stories are as acute as the smell of wreaths and garlands; I lie awake at night and wonder about them, walking their lives just out of sight in the ancient glabrous dark, oblivious—maybe not oblivious. It's communing with auras, shades, living ghosts . . . A bar girl in the Russian enclave of Kaliningrad who asked to see my passport and held it to her nose. Closing her eyes she sighed: "Ah, the smell of freedom." . . . The Tanzanian Masai herdsman who escorted me through the bush at dusk with his red toga and broad-bladed buffalo spear because the lions were hunting. We'd been drinking warm cows' blood in his kraal. "I'm not only a cattle farmer," he said, "I'm an English teacher as well. Do you know the works of James Hadley Chase?" . . . The Afghan mujahideen fighter I came upon in a narrow street in Peshawar—I caught his pale, fierce eye as he strode purposefully toward me. I knew there was something wrong; this was the beginning of the Afghan war, the RAF were bombing Kabul. As we drew parallel, he darted and grabbed me, slamming me against a wall. I tensed for the feeling of the cold steel between my ribs and stared into the impervious raptor face. Out of the corner of my eye, I caught the rim of a cartwheel passing within inches of my head. He had just saved my life. But he knew what I was thinking . . . he let me go, took a step back, and touched his heart with his right hand . . .

The beautiful Sudanese refugee who had lost her family, whose husband was dead and who had just given birth to twins—little boys, perfect, healthy. They lay one on each side of her in the iron hospital bed, silent. She didn't look at them or touch them, just stared at something invisible in the distance with the blank face of stoic Africa. She refused to feed them, wishing her only children dead rather than having to struggle in the meager, miserable, damned world she had to offer them. The nurses and doctors begged and implored and prayed for her to pick up her children, but she wouldn't. Unable to kill or to give life, she hung on the wire of untenable choices, her bright nightdress wet with milk . . .

My Japanese interpreter in a restaurant. I asked him to teach me Japanese table manners. "No need," he said. I insisted. "No, no, really . . . No need." Please. "I couldn't." Look, I insisted, it's my job, I need to know. "No," he said emphatically. "I couldn't. I can't. You wouldn't understand. We have all"—he waved at the rest of the diners—"agreed not to notice you. We don't see your clumsiness and ugliness. It is like the paper walls, we hear but we don't listen. We look but we don't see." . . . The creative writing lecturer in a bookshop in Santa Barbara who'd written a "how to write" book called *Let the Crazy Child Write!* and who said, "We each are three people—

a head editor, a heart writer and a crazy child. The crazy child says, Imagine a three-legged dog, and then says, Imagine a three-legged dog running. You can't, can you? You can't imagine a three-legged dog running? Isn't that great?" It was like an insistent pop tune. I couldn't imagine anything but a three-legged dog running, round and round, yapping, "Isn't it great, isn't it great." . . .

The boy who sidled up to me in the lobby of the Hotel Nacional in Havana and asked if I wanted to buy a bootleg tape of Cuban music with "Guantanamera," the much-derided and -repeated folk song whose lyrics were written by José Martí, an exiled journalist and poet, an agrarian communist, one of the founders of the revolutionary movement to free Cuba. He invaded the country in a hopelessly romantic gesture and died trying to storm a police station. But his writing was the basis of the Cuban revolution, and the words of "Guantanamera" are beautiful and elegiac and sad, and in Havana as insistent as a three-legged dog. I didn't want the tape, but I asked the boy if he would like dinner and to tell me about his life here. He'd never eaten a steak before. All his school friends had piled onto an oil drum raft during the small window that a petulant Castro had offered to people who wanted to leave Cuba to get to Florida, ninety miles away. The boy had got as far as the shore, but didn't go with them because he lost his nerve and worried about his mother. "It was the worst decision of my life," he said. Now he spent hours on his bed feeling his life drift away and listened to American radio and dreamed about the parallel existence that might have been his in Amer-

ica. "I know all the state capitals, really all of them. I look at
the map every night and plan the journeys I will make." Okay,
New York? "Albany." California? "Sacramento." Kansas?
"Topeka." Delaware? "Dover." Alaska? "Juneau." Kentucky?
"Frankfort." . . .

A hunter who after a long trek through the bush said, "I bet
you can't hit that baboon from here." The one reading the
paper? "Yep." . . . The Rohingya refugee who had been in a
camp in Bangladesh for twenty years, whom Burma had made
stateless, gently unwrapping a handkerchief that contained the
frail slips and frayed and folded slithers of paper—letters,
passes, bills—that were the only things that proved he'd ever
existed. "Someone," he said, "has written my name. There is a
government stamp. I was a person. When I die, someone will
have to write down that they buried me," and he wept, the
tears falling on the delicate faint leaves of an invisible life . . .
And the very chic blond guide in Reykjavík when I was doing a
story about the banking collapse. She was diligent, direct, effi-
cient and had strong opinions. At the end of the trip I paid her
and thanked her. She put the cash in her pocket, looked at me
and said in a loud, clear, singsong Scandi accent, "You know
you're a cunt?" Tom laughed so much I thought he'd wet himself.

The last of the things I like about journalism is that it is
ephemeral. We write for deadlines, not posterity. Both our triumphs and pratfalls are lining the parrot's cage by Wednesday,
and no one remembers journalists. Our bylines pass with
the news. Name five famous dead hacks? They're all likely to
be memorable for something else—Kipling, Twain, Dickens,

Hemingway, H. M. Stanley, Mussolini. We look, we write, we file and depart, leaving nothing much behind. Andreas Whittam Smith, the first editor of *The Independent*, said that journalism was a trade not a profession (except in America, where they call themselves "men of letters"). We are like monumental masons working on medieval cathedrals; we carve our gargoyles and inscriptions and then we vanish, but the church remains—what it stands for, its litany, its service, its round of reading and commenting—while the men who made and maintained it are dust. I find that comforting.

13

Nicola has just asked me if I'm going to write about being a parent. I wasn't. As Tolstoy would have undoubtedly got round to saying, "All parents are smug in the same way." There are few things as gratingly annoying as listening to people talk about their children. When I take our twins to school, I watch the parents chat to each other, the expressions are always the same. The one talking has a look of animated, amused enthusiasm. The one listening wears the expression of someone in a traffic jam. The rule of talking about your children is that you can only ever do it to other people with children . . . people without children who say they are interested in yours are lying. And you must never forget that this is a verbal cricket match . . . you get an innings, and then they get an innings, and their job is to get you out as soon as possible and then stay in for as long as possible. Talk about children is a phatic communion; like birdsong, it's simply trilling: "I'm here, I'm here, I'm here . . . I have eggs."

I realize that mostly I still think of myself as a child of parents rather than a parent of children. I have been a child longer than I've been a parent, but being a parent of children is so much more fun and engrossing and profound than being a child to your parents. The biggest thing that happens in any life is the life of your children. No tragedy or triumph can compare with the tragedies or triumphs of them. I have never felt such churning fury as when I thought my children were being bullied; or such steepling pride as when they do something kind or clever. No award, no medal, no mountain peak, no victory could compare with the moment you become a parent. I remember exactly where I was when I learned I was going to be a father for the first time, and exactly what I felt—a stupefied disbelief, a numb terror. I was thirty-eight. And there was in the seven years of my sober life a handful of things that I knew to be home truths: I would never play golf, I would never be a soldier, I would never own property, I would never join a political party, I would never wear a T-shirt with whimsical writing on it, I would never eat pizza with pineapple and I would never be a father. I was plainly, genetically, unequipped to parent anyone; I had made such a patently bad job of looking after myself, I couldn't be trusted with children. When I learned I was going to be a father, I was lying on a mattress in my mother's flat with Lily the dog, who couldn't get upstairs anymore and was inclemently incontinent. I spent the next eight months in a state of underground terror. My panic was like the French Resistance, it pretended to be just normal worry during the day and then would become full-on panic at night, blowing up resolve, silently strangling intentions, sowing the propaganda of doubt. I lay awake thinking of all the things I could do for a child and all the things that could go wrong. I didn't say any of this out loud, because obviously Amber had to worry about all this stuff that I worried about, whilst also being pregnant . . . and with the added worry that she had me as a partner. The one thing I never doubted was that she would be a good mother, and twenty-four years later there's not a single day when she hasn't been. I didn't go to the hospital when Flora was born. I think it was because Amber said I wouldn't be a help. She says it was because I said I wouldn't be a help. I got a call early in the morning from a midwife to tell me that I should get on a bus. By the time I got there, everything would be finished. I was told to wait in a corridor with another pacing man, and then a door opened a few inches and an Irish accent said, "Give it a couple of minutes while we make mum presentable, and here's your daughter," and this swaddled child, eyes closed, with a look of deep thought, was put into my arms. I'd never held a new baby before. She fitted naturally and comfortably into the crook of my arm, like the missing piece of a puzzle. I stared at the small pink face and my head filled with a grace, a golden blessing. I had a marvelous godmother, Joan, who'd been a nurse. She was Yorkshire, no-nonsense, firm and kind and devout. She said that a surprising number of parents worried about being able to love their children, but she always told them, "Don't worry, every child comes with its own parcel of love." I thought this was syrupy, trite, a nursery truism until I held this little bundle. I've never before been conscious of falling in love in real time as it happened—love is something you recognize in retrospect, the thing that grows, that is painful and uncomfortable and unstoppable. It comes from other things. But this, this was nature and nurture all together. I knew absolutely with perfect clarity that I would love this little girl all my life without hesitation or question. I also knew that it would all be all right—the worries, the projected calamities—they would all be all right. We would manage. Better than that, we would flourish.

I went to church, St. Mary Abbots, and I sat at the back. There was no one else there, and I read the Collect for that week: "God for whom we watch and wait, you sent John the Baptist to prepare the way of your Son, give us courage to speak the truth, to hunger for justice and to suffer for the cause of right." The Evangelist that lives in the wilderness on wild honey, who's half mad, who points the insistent finger in Grünewald's Crucifixion—"It is not me, it is he who comes after." So Flora's second name was chosen. Evangeline.

I said that the hinge of my life was before and after drink and drugs. The second chance. But there is another fold, deeper and more profound: before and after my children. The birth of Flora changed everything. Two years later there was Alasdair. I wasn't there for his birth either, I was looking after Flora, desperately worried that she'd be upset by the arrival of another child demanding her mother's attention. We went to the hospital together to pick her baby. She said she wanted a brother. So I took her to the maternity unit with its rows of cribs and new babies and she pointed to a pleasant-looking little chap who was my Alasdair, and again I felt the grace of love and the sense of rightness. And then later, with Nicola, the twins came.

And I was there for them. I hadn't meant to be, but the doctor said just pop in for a couple of moments, and did I bring a CD? asked the nurse. I didn't know that babies had to come with a sound track. And then presto, with the dramatic efficiency of a birthday magician, the gore-striped child was lifted over the curtain that had been drawn over Nicola's lower half like a Punch and Judy set—a little girl. And immediately afterward, a little boy. Edith and Isaac, and the now unsurprising but still ecstatic feeling of not falling but filling with love. Edith, after Nicola's grandmother, and Isaac, Hebrew for the gift of laughter. Sarah, Abraham's wife, laughs when she is told she will give birth: she thinks she will never conceive. Isaac also got Mungo, the familiar or pet name of Saint Kentigern that means "my dear one" or "mate." Edith got Lara, which Nicola liked, and in a postnatal reverie as I walked into the registry office to make them official, I added Pyramus and Thisbe. I wanted something Shakespearean that wasn't Beatrice and Benedick. *Pyramus and Thisbe* is the play within a play in *A Midsummer Night's Dream*. A story from Persia of star-crossed lovers that may be the origin of *Romeo and Juliet*. Thisbe is also by panto tradition the name of one of the ugly sisters.

All the way through their childhoods, other parents have clucked and said, Ooh, look out, you're about to enter the terrible twos, or the fraught fours, or the naughty nines, or appalling adolescence. But so far there hasn't been a day I wouldn't joyfully have again, and that's about as smug as I can manage.

Am I a good father? It's not for me to say. That's their prerogative. I try hard: everything I've done after Flora's birth has been made with the knowledge that I have a family and the responsibility of them. It certainly made me work harder than I ever did before and it provoked a new level of anxiety. When Ali was tiny, a woman stopped me in a shop and said what a lovely child. He had a mole on his face, he used to call it his Dalmatian. "Do you worry about the mark?" the woman said. Yes, a bit. And she looked at me and added, "You know, there are two types of parent—those that enjoy their children, and those that worry about them." I remember that ruefully because I enjoy my children hugely, but my anxiety for them is also enormous. And whilst worry is external, based on projected outcomes, anxiety is internal, like mistletoe, it finds a host to grow on. I have found that anxiety can be hideously debilitating, seriously depressing, and mine, always, nests on the children, particularly if I can't get hold of them. Since my brother's vanishing, I have a panicky need to know where everyone is. That's enough unsolicited kids' stuff. I'm also aware that their lives are theirs, they don't belong to me to parade as an extension of mine. There is one bit of paternal pride I'll add—I've always been a ten-quid dad. There are few lumps in family life that can't be flattened with the judicious ten-pound note. Ten quid to tidy your room, to say sorry, to admit I'm right. It's not really ten quid, it's a MacGuffin, a prop, a wand, a time-out, a ruse, a high-horse dismounter, a secret door in the wall your back's up against, a face-saver. It allows everyone to walk away and get on without the row grumbling on or going nuclear. Flora says it's a really awful way to be a parent, and that it'll turn her small brother and sister into avaricious pawnbrokers—well, it didn't turn her or her brother into one. They are remarkably unmaterialistic. I casually asked Ali the other day if he had any plans for a career, he's twenty-two. He smiled and put his hands on my shoulders—he's taller than me now—and said, "Dad, Dad, not really my sort of thing, is it?" I couldn't have been prouder of him.

Okay, that really is the end of the smugness. And that wasn't what I'm proud of. I'm proud that none of my children or either of their mothers has had to deal with me being drunk or out of it. The constant fear is that this is a hereditary condition, that I might pass on the faulty gene, the receptor that doesn't have an off switch. But at least I won't compound the inheritance with learned behavior. Not both nurture and nature. Three of them have got varying degrees of dyslexia, they have me to thank for that. And I have made three unbreakable family rules—no tattoos, no motorbikes and no heroin. The heroin is negotiable, I know what to do about heroin.

And then there's God. I am a reluctant Christian. I was once interviewed by Lynn Barber for *The Guardian*, and I told her I was a Christian, but not a homosexual . . . she didn't believe either. "You can't be a Christian," she said, in her parlor maid's voice, "you just can't." Well, I can, that's the thing with religion. Absolutely anyone can. "But you're not remotely Christian," she continued. "It's another contrarian affectation." What, like bow ties? "Yes." I wish it were. Having a dose of religion, in my milieu, at this time, is as awkward and inconvenient as not having it in seventeenth-century Norwich. It would be so much more socially easy to be a vain fashion atheist. I was brought up by atheists. I honestly thought I was immune to religiosity. And I didn't catch it in a Methodist way after signing the pledge. I began to have vague spiritual unease because of art at the Slade, and that really was contrarian. I'd go and sit in the back of churches and feel wordlessly moved. There was a family friend, an Irish Jesuit and university professor who occasionally took me out to lunch and I'd confide in him. He was a radical libertarian theologist, which was exciting; and he said, if at all possible, religion was something to be avoided. Who would willingly lumber themselves with a book full of medieval rules, superstitions and the possibility of an eternity's agony by choice? Far better, he said, to adopt a general humanitarian goodness, be thoughtful, charitable and kind, and trust in the benevolence of Providence to see you all right. He pointed out that statistically religious belief had no actuarial benefits: you didn't get to live longer, or have less cancer; religious people didn't have prettier spouses, politer children, more sex . . . quite possibly less sex . . . nicer offices or better weather. They did, on the other hand, get guilt (point of order here, it's the Catholics and Jews who get guilt, Protestants and Muslims get shame). And of course remorse.

You don't really believe that do you? I said. "Adrian, I wish to God I did, but I can't because the space is already filled with a belief in God." I think I've got it too, I said. "Which flavor are you?" Well, that's rather the thing, I've got a formless faith. He said, "If you want my advice, go with what's closest to home. Faith is ethereal, the practice of faith is cultural. If you become a Zoroastrian or a follower of Cao Dai, a marvelous Vietnamese Christianity that believes Mohammed, Moses, Louis Pasteur, Shakespeare, Lenin and Victor Hugo are all saints, then you're going to have to learn a lot of stuff . . . and get over a whole lot of other stuff before you get to the good stuff, and it'll have very little to do with your soul. Weren't you baptized into the Church of Scotland? I'd stick with Protestantism. Actually, I think it rather suits you . . . low to middle. Anglo-Catholicism would bring out the worst in you, all the dressing up would get out of control and you'd become an architectural pedant doing brass rubbings." And so that's essentially what I am—a lazy, middle-range Protestant with a mildly pedantic crush on the King James Version and the Book of Common Prayer. I think William Tyndale is one of the greatest heroes of our country, even if you don't believe an inch of religion. The translator of the Bible into English taught himself five languages and was cussed and determined and difficult and truly egalitarian and said, "I defy the Pope and all his laws. If God spare my life ere many years, I will cause the boy that drives the plow to know more of the scriptures than you." And that voice from five hundred years ago, that tone, is still instantly recognizable as dissenting, argumentative British of the most laudable cut. It's not just that he'll teach the plowboy to know scripture, but to know more scriptures than you do. I'm not the sort of Christian that atheists or even other Christians want to argue with, I'm not a Southern Baptist or a creationist, I don't believe that the Bible is history or literal, I don't think homosexuality is a sin or that it's fine to keep slaves, I don't care if your garments are made of more than one material, I don't hold strong opinions about the eating of owls or eagles, and I plainly don't care about not selling newspapers on Sundays thereby defiling the Sabbath. I have no argument with Darwin—though I might have with Newton: his science is marvelous, but most of his life was actually spent doing some very bizarre theology, not least searching for the philosopher's stone to turn base metal into gold. I don't believe that any sort of sex is sinful—it might be illegal or uncomfortable, but that's temporal not spiritual, and I think anyone should be able to marry anyone and possibly anything. Why shouldn't you marry a tree or a chicken or a Teasmade if you're truly in love with each other? What do I think God is? Anything it wants to be . . . It's God. It might be a pantheon, it might be a formless power surge. In my rickety belief, there is far, far more unknowing than knowing; as Kierkegaard put it over coffee and cake: The only rational, thoughtful, intelligent reaction to religion is masses of doubt, tempered with incredulity . . . He did *what* after three days? It's a bit like a Bob Newhart telephone sketch: "Hi, Jonah baby, it's been an age . . . Really? I'm not gonna believe it? Try me . . . You were playing dice on a ship and it got a bit rough and the sailor said that it was your fault . . . and what did you say, Jonah? . . . You said it probably was your fault and they should throw you overboard. That was rash, Joe . . . Can you swim? . . . I thought not. So they threw you overboard . . . you sank, right? Oh, the sea was calm . . . whoa, weird. So did they pick you up again? Okay, this is the weird bit . . . How big? Really, really big . . . Well, you're not a small man, Joe . . . Did it chew? . . . Just swallowed, that was lucky . . . And then what, Joe? . . . It was dark, I bet it was. How long were you inside? . . . Jeez, three days . . . that's a long time to be sushi. And you prayed . . . Yeah, I bet. What did you pray for, Joe? To make the fish puke, right? . . . No, no, I see where you're coming from . . . better than out the other end . . . I bet he did . . . I don't expect he's had many prayers to make fish sick . . . it'll have stood out. So the fish barfed . . .

What's it like being vomit, Joe? . . . Never mind . . . Where are you now? . . . Nineveh . . . That's a shit hole. And what are you doing there? . . . Okay . . . Telling them to wear sackcloth and ashes . . . including the animals . . . or the Lord will smite them . . . So the fish thing didn't improve your temper any, Joe? Same old Jonah . . . No, no, of course, I believe every word . . . I'm evangelical, I've done the Alpha Course."

So religion is extended periods of doubt with occasional flashes of faith that are feelings rather than instructions. I've never had a prayer specifically answered, but then I've never had one officially turned down, either. It's the bright, intense moments of belief, like lightning in a dark night, that keep me hooked. And I like the culture of my Christianity, the buildings, the art, the music, all the kit, the holidays, the cakes, the civilization of God. I don't know that I see it or experience it any differently from or more intensely than humanists, it belongs to them as much as to me, but I find its edifice and ecstasy inspiring and encouraging. Belief isn't instead of empiricism, faith and knowledge aren't mutually exclusive, the rational world doesn't replace a spiritual one, they live in parallel, they are the walls and the windows of our existence. Without the wall there is no structure, without the window no vision, no light, you choose which is which. To deny one would be stupid, to deny the other, insensitive. I have no desire to recruit or convince others: religion is frankly embarrassing. If you can avoid it, good for you. I don't think it matters if a hundred or a billion people believe in God. I made sure my children know the Lord's Prayer, because it's useful to know at least one prayer, like carrying a handkerchief, but after that it's up to them. Flora had a few years of following a bishop around with a candle and writing the Sunday-school nativity play. She studied theology and philosophy at university, came back after her first year and said, "Sorry, Dad, but I don't believe in God." That's okay. What matters is that you believe in you, and that whatever it is, God still believes in you.

Most Christmases I read a lesson at a carol service held at a small Moravian church. The Moravians were an early Reformation sect that sprang from the teaching of John Wycliffe and the Lollards. They were persecuted at the end of the Thirty Years' War, and a number of them made their way to London to be a missionary church in America. As they waited for a ship, they set up a chapel in the East End, and a Church of England vicar used to stop by and sit in on services—he liked their simplicity, the use of music and hymn singing, and he started to do something similar in his own church. He was John Wesley, and it was the beginning of the nonconformist movement, the Methodist church. The Moravians got their ship and set off for the New World and a century later they returned to London—now mostly West Indian—and it's still a church full of song and simplicity.

AN ANALYST TOLD ME she had a theory that anxiety might be an early conditioned response to boredom, that there are some children who really, really can't deal with boredom and their attempts to overcome it create anxiety, which of course, is never boring. An inability or a clumsiness to live with boredom is also often an early symptom—or perhaps a cause—of addiction. After thirty years of being sober and clean, I am no clearer on whether my drinking and drug taking was a cause or a symptom. Did I get depressed and anxious because I drank? Or did I drink because I was depressed and anxious? *In vino veritas*, or is it just the booze talking? I had half a hope that writing this memoir might bring me closer to an understanding of the pathology of my particular collection of symptoms and circumstances, but it turns out that it's still the same cigar box of old photos, postcards, protest buttons, get-well cards, wedding invitations, Dear John notes, letters, reports and pressed flowers that don't quite amount to a coherent story and don't have a moral. And probably, it doesn't matter. I misused a life for thirty years and I had thirty more of a second chance that I used better, though not as well as I might have. I've had a family I never thought I would have, I fell in love with a handful of women who are all still my friends and whom I never cease to love. I found a corner to work in where I never imagined there would be space for me and I've made a living by watching television, eating in restaurants and traveling to see things that are generally only shown to soldiers, missionaries or journalists.

WE STARTED WITH THE TWO BOATS—which one to stop. The answer now, it seems, is, we should stop them both and get the people inside to come aboard with you. And then you must pick up more people as you go along, the lost, the becalmed, the desperate, the ones thrown overboard, the garrulous, the fun and the beautiful. Like Odysseus', the voyage is the adventure. We are all in the same boat, all refugees from the past trying to find a home.

ACKNOWLEDGMENTS

Thank you to Alan Samson, Celia Hayley, Michelle Klepper, Ed Victor, Charlie Brotherstone, Lucinda McNeile, Simon Wright and Linden Lawson.

ABOUT THE AUTHOR

A.A. Gill was born in Edinburgh. He is the author of *A.A. Gill Is Away*, *The Angry Island*, *Previous Convictions*, *Table Talk*, *Paper View*, *A.A. Gill Is Further Away* and *To America with Love*, as well as two novels. He is the TV and restaurant critic and regular features writer for *The Sunday Times*, a columnist for *Esquire*, and a contributor to *Australian Gourmet Traveller*. He lives in London and spends much of his year traveling. He has been nominated for more awards than he has won.